ECO-SPIRITUALITY IN THE 21ST CENTURY

ReVisioning Nature, Community, and Connection FOR A BETTER TOMORROW

REDFeather® MIND | BODY | SPIRIT
An Imprint of Schiffer Publishing, Ltd.

Dana O'Driscoll
& Nate Summers

Contents

Acknowledgments

Dana would like to thank her gnomish whimsical partner, Robert Pacitti, for creating a home both to explore these ideas and get them written. She would also like to thank her goose flock for their ongoing joy, inspiration, and love. She thanks all the plants, stones, insects, animals, and rivers, and the beautiful Allegheny Mountains, who serve as her most-important teachers. She is very grateful to Lillian Wolf, who has deepened her understanding of animism and taught her Indigenous ways of interacting in the world. She also is grateful to her many teachers and mentors who have taught her the ideas, ways of thinking, philosophies, and practices brought to life in this book: John Michael Greer, Sara Greer, Jim McDonald, Kay Caffaso, Jason Drevanak, Pandora Thomas, Deanne Bednar, and Lisa DiPiano. She is highly inspired by the many incredible people doing good healing in the world, such as Linda Jackson, Sue Morris, and the folks at Dancing Rabbit Ecovillage. And finally, to her wonderful family for their support, joy, and creative inspiration.

Nate would like to acknowledge and thank the long line of teachers and mentors who are the transmitters of various lineages that have informed this book and the work he does in the world. This includes but is not limited to Jon Young, John Five Bears White, Gilbert Walking Bull, Zhi Cheng, Tony Ten Fingers, Chris Kenworthy, Mary Stuart, Mick Dodge, Jake Swamp, and many others. He also wants to share a heartfelt thanks and acknowledgment of support from his family, including his children, Katie, Tara, and Orion, and his loving partner, Karen Joy Fletcher.

Endorsements

Eco-Spirituality in the 21st Century is a beautifully comprehensive guide to healing our relationship to everything. Within you'll find the path to discovering the essential knowledge, skills, and tools to empower you to lead a rich and regenerative life. Following the well-laid-out framework of this book has the potential to bring you true wealth that will ripple out into the world all around you—near and far, present and future.

—Liz Neves, author of *Northeast Medicinal Plants: Identify, Harvest, and Use 111 Wild Herbs for Health and Wellness* (Timber Press)

If you are one of the many who feel overwhelmed, in despair, and confounded by the state of our world in these challenging times, read this book! If you care deeply for the earth and want to make a difference in life and legacy, read this book. In these pages, you will find a medicinal weaving of insight, wisdom, and grounded action to remember our way forward as stewards and healers of the earth.

—Fearn Lickfield, chief of the Green Mountain Druid Order, and steward of Dreamland Sanctuary

Eco-Spirituality in the 21st Century is a much-needed book of hope in a troubled world. It challenges us to craft new visions and to tell empowering stories about a sustainable future for our planet. With its 7 Key principles for positive change and with storytelling and practical tools, it explores deeply and soulfully the role we might play in manifesting those visions for the good of all. As we reach for new ways to be, this book gifts us with a clarity and optimism about the power we all have to create meaningful and long-lasting change.

—Philip Carr-Gomm, author of *Druid Mysteries*, *What Do Druids Believe?*, and *The Druid Way*

Rewilding
Regeneration
Resilience
Reenchantment
Revisioning
Reconnection
Respect

Introduction

With Dana O'Driscoll and Nate Summers

"We have to tell a better story . . . ," the words from Nate's colleague Gene Tagaban hit hard initially, and over the next few years, their importance and impact kept unfolding. Gene is a traditional storyteller, mentor, and Raven Dancer of Native Alaskan, Cherokee, and Filipino descent. His long, dark hair streaked with gray, and his wise and intelligent eyes are only part of his charisma. He's a compelling speaker, storyteller, and healer. Nate and Gene's conversation was about how we could really make a difference in the world in the face of overwhelming global climate change, political divisiveness, economic instability, and a world that seemed increasingly fragmented.

Gene is a storyteller at heart, but he's also adept at getting people to tell *their* stories. In fact, just like other healer/storytellers of similar ilk such as Cherokee/Lakota scholar and healer Lewis Mehl-Madrona, Gene uses storytelling and people's own stories as a way to unlock new ways of seeing, experiencing, and being in the world. *A new reality is created through this powerful work.* Sometimes Gene dresses in incredibly elaborate, beautiful regalia with a huge raven headdress, hand-carved wooden wings, and blue-black tassels in order to become Raven and dance a story into being that has been handed down through countless generations echoing cosmological and mythological truths. Other times he simply gets an audience to open up, laugh, and just consider the story of where they came from. Whatever the case, the storytelling arts, techniques, and ways Gene uses are literally quite magical. Storytelling is a magical act; it always has been. And some would say it is the most powerful form of magic around as it helps create and invoke a different reality.

If that's the case, then the stories we are telling ourselves and the magic around them are certainly weaving a powerful field of darkness, despair, and dystopia. In fact, one could say that the immense popularity of the genres of *grimdark, post-apocalypticism,* and *dystopia* in the world of books, film, and entertainment are literally creating a worse world every day. We have to wonder, would the concepts present in *1984*[1] be as visible today if the book hadn't been so well read? Did George Orwell manifest these concepts as a magical act, or were these already present and he simply channeled what was already coming into focus? Perhaps it is a sign of the times that most of what has been produced via mass media in the twentieth and twenty-first centuries is rather dystopian and chilling. In addition, you have to wonder about the effects of extremely popular dystopian books and shows like *Game of Thrones, The Handmaid's Tale, The Walking Dead,* and *Breaking Bad.* Are they part of what is creating the divisiveness, discord, and ugliness all around us? Words have power. Words can shape reality and incite people to action or cause chaos and destruction. So, the question is: what are the stories we are telling ourselves, and what is the vision we are collectively creating?

We both independently noticed this dystopian narrative happening around us. In fact, the general dark tone of modern life actually generated and started conversations that led to this book. We both had a sense that the stories we were telling as a human civilization were creating a field of doom and gloom. It's almost as if we were all under a particular kind of spell . . .

The book your hold in your hand is a specific remedy against this strange miasma of reality-distorting and hope-crushing grimness. It is a grimoire to dispel a dark future, and a magical act designed to help us create and reveal a new future freeing us from the dystopian world we have all woken up to. While no one can dispute the importance and value of the message of works like *1984* and *A Brave New World,* we really don't want to live in a world that increasingly resembles those stories.

If storytelling is one of the oldest and most powerful forms of magic, it's time to tell a new story, a story of hope laced with solutions, ideas, and inspiration. That is, let us *revision* the future. Visioning can be one of the most powerful statements and forms of rebellion in the face of forces that would encourage the status quo as a way to profit, dominate, and keep extracting from the world. Let's instead weave a more hopeful, greener, regenerative future for ourselves and for the future generations of this planet both human and nonhuman. Let us bring about a better paradigm and vision for the future. But, how? The ideas presented in this book serves as one answer.

IMPETUS FOR THE WORK AHEAD AND ABOUT US

Right now, humans and all life on Earth are facing an ecological and social crisis of unprecedented proportions. As this crisis unfolds, many people are turning to nature spirituality and nature-based skills and returning to nature in various forms as a way forward. In the wake of the global pandemic and with the ramping up of extreme weather events and climate change, a record number of people are recognizing that they want to connect more deeply with nature and make other fundamental shifts in their lives. For example, the Ancient Order of Druids in America[2] (of which Dana serves as the Grand Archdruid) has increased membership by over 200 percent in the three pandemic years alone—and these numbers are similar for other Druid and nature-based orders and continue into the present. More people—particularly young people—are getting outside, reconnecting with nature, and wanting to build a meaningful nature-based spirituality than ever before. However, the tools and methods for reconnecting with nature and building a nature-based spirituality that will sustain us into the future are lacking or are found in piecemeal ways. For one, many of the foundational books on nature spirituality were written before the current crisis took shape, or they are rooted in outdated formal magical traditions or "feel good" books designed only to support individuals' practices. But for this new generation of seekers, nature spirituality isn't just about meditating in the woods or scripted rituals—it is about a response and desire to live differently in order to address the crisis of our age. As leaders in our respective communities, we've been working to respond to these needs and doing our own reVisioning of what a responsive, twenty-first-century nature spirituality would look like to help create a better future.

Before we connected, we both arrived at very similar conclusions: that the current tools in the nature spirituality community were insufficient and that we needed new tools and methods for visioning and daily living in nature-connected ways. As we began to talk about the possibility of this book, we discovered we had a complementary set of skills and teaching experiences that would allow us to craft the book we felt needed to be written—a book that neither of us could have written alone. Because of this, our bookend chapters are written collaboratively (this introduction and chapter 7, "ReVisioning"), but the remainder are written primarily by only one of us, drawing upon our unique skill sets. We now share a bit about each of us.

Dana O'Driscoll has been an animist Druid for twenty years and currently serves as the Grand Archdruid of the Ancient Order of Druids in America (AODA), a well-known Druid order focusing on wild-crafted, biocentric nature spirituality. Through her leadership, AODA has been shifting focus to engage in some of the practices in this book through group-based ceremonies for land healing and blessing, reconnection with nature, and regenerative approaches. Dana also lives in a region of the United States that has been pillaged by four centuries of resource extraction, most recently fracking, mountaintop removal, deforestation, acid-mine drainage, coal mining, and much more. These experiences led her to a lifelong study of regenerative land-healing techniques (both ceremonial and physical). Thus, she is a certified permaculture designer and certified permaculture teacher, a wild-food/foraging teacher, an herbalist, and a nature-based artist. She lives a regenerative, care-oriented lifestyle as a homesteader and wild tender on 5 acres in western Pennsylvania with her partner and a host of feathered and furred friends. Her goal on the land is to learn how to work with nature to create healthy and rich ecosystems, refuges for life, and a better tomorrow.

Nate Summers has been a survival skills instructor for over twenty years, with a background in anthropology, ecology, naturalist skills, and natural medicine. He taught and directed at the Wilderness Awareness School for over fifteen years and has served as faculty for the Desert Institute of Healing Arts and the Asian Institute of Medical Studies and as adjunct faculty for Prescott College. Nate's passions include ethnobotany, natural mentoring, hunter-gatherer childhoods, natural movement, and herbal medicine. He is a well-known teacher and author in the field, as well as being a naturalist guide leading people from all over the country and all over the world on expeditions to Mount Rainier, Mount St. Helens, and Olympic National Park.

In order to accomplish *Eco-Spirituality in the 21st Century*, we pull from our own considerable skill sets, including druidry, ancestral skills, earth skills, wilderness survival skills, deep nature connection, permaculture, regenerative agriculture, wild-food foraging, rewilding, herbalism, leading and writing ceremonies, and nature spirituality. By drawing upon a wide variety of disciplines, we offer a comprehensive eco-spirituality that uniquely speaks to our present challenges and future. We also seek and draw upon the wisdom of enduring communities, traditions, and cultures by privileging Indigenous voices and practices that are open as much as possible.

Because we belong to a diverse number of communities, we see the seeds for a better future already planted in many of the communities and wisdom from which we draw this book. This new paradigm for the future isn't unique to a single community or place, but it is emerging in very diverse communities. The themes of this new vision—the 7 R's we present in this book—are not any single person's vision, but a confluence of so many different people and communities learning how to reconnect and how to heal the earth, and to offer an alternative to the current vision of the future. In this book, we are working to give it voice and structure, but it belongs to all of us. And also, as we will explore by drawing upon Indigenous wisdom, this "new" paradigm is not new at all. It is a return to older lifeways and understandings, understandings held by many groups of people across time, particularly tied to Indigenous ways of knowing and being in the world (and if we all go far back enough, we are indigenous to somewhere).

HOPE FOR THE FUTURE AND A NEW PARADIGM EMERGING

We could certainly fill this book with everything that is going wrong right now. In the briefest description, our ecological, social, financial, and every other system that we depend on to survive is in what Donnela Meadows, Jorgen Randers, and Dennis Meadows have been describing as "overshoot" since the early 1970s.[3] Overshoot is when natural limits are radically exceeded, which creates stresses that begin to slow and stop existing systems that depend on growth. In the case of right now, humanity has caused the entire planetary system to be in "overshoot," which means that we're demanding more resources than the carrying capacity of the planet can support. This is leading to a wide range of issues such as climate change, the ongoing sixth mass extinction, societal breakdowns, economic turmoil, social and community upheaval, and so forth. These issues aren't going to go away. We could spend all of our time talking about these issues, but plenty of books, United Nations reports, and so forth have already outlined the problems in stark detail. While these difficult realities are in our present, we choose to live in *hope* and not in *fear*. What this book offers is a vision that takes us out of overshoot and back into a place of balance by connecting with nature, ourselves, spirit, and our communities.

Helping all of us become good ancestors is one of the reasons we wrote *Eco-Spirituality in the 21st Century*—to reach this new generation of people looking to practice a meaningful, connected, and future-oriented nature spirituality and to offer all of us the tools for visioning a better world. Because at this point, we all want to be *part of the solution*, and we need a whole set of new tools to do this work.

And, as we'll explore more in chapter 7, we recognize that we are in the process of experiencing a new paradigm being born. This paradigm is a direct response to the systems described above that have brought our planet to the brink of ecological and societal collapse. It doesn't have a name, and you aren't going to hear about it on the nightly news. And yet, it is being born in millions of places all over this beautiful planet: in community gardens, in nature spirituality events, in bushcraft events and herbalism schools, in permaculture design certificate programs, in natural-pigment foraging, and in communities of nature spirituality. And for many of us born into these destructive systems, we are eager to embrace a nature-honoring and care-oriented way of being.

A big part of what we are doing is trying to build on the philosophies shared by Robin Wall Kimmerer in *Braiding Sweetgrass*.[4] Kimmerer describes reindigenizing, or becoming what she calls "naturalized to place" and establishing reciprocal relationships of kinship between humans and nature. When we reindigenize to our local ecosystems, we can learn how to live in balance, to tend our ecosystems, and to recognize that we are part of nature. This is a huge part of the new paradigm that is emerging, and more and more people are taking up this work. Thankfully, Indigenous teachers (some of our own and public ones such as Robin Wall Kimmerer and Tyson Yunkaporta) are providing us with accessible, open philosophies for how to do this. Thus, one of the things we work to do is to bring together open-source Indigenous teachings with growing nature-based spirituality movements in North America and a host of practical nature-oriented skills. Thus, in responding to these needs, we've crafted a book that weaves a new kind of eco-spirituality that deeply connects you with meaningful practices that create a brighter vision for the future, that lets you get dirty and be present in nature, and that gives you powerful, flexible frameworks for your own ceremonial creation. The book allows you to craft spiritual and sacred practices to things you are already doing with nature, such as wild-food foraging, organic gardening, and herbalism. It allows you to establish kinship relationships with the living earth in reverent, reciprocal, and care-oriented ways. Through these kinship relations and reindigenizing, we choose hope and not fear. We choose care. We choose to learn how to be better ancestors and leave a better ancestral legacy than the one we have been given.

ECO-SPIRITUALITY BOOK OVERVIEW

Eco-Spirituality in the 21st Century offers a new vision for nature spirituality by drawing upon both ancient, ancestral connections and visioning a wide set of practices, meditations, and ceremonies for the future. We recognize that if humanity is to survive and thrive in the future, we need to re-envision our entire approach to human life and eco-spirituality is at the core of that approach. Thus, we offer a grand vision of seven principles—what we call the 7 R's—for re-envisioning humans' relationship with the living earth. This book is a unique offering that goes beyond "surface" spirituality and encourages readers to return to their ancestral roots to envision a better tomorrow, weaving past, present, and future. *Eco-Spirituality in the 21st Century* is a guide for how to create frameworks for living that promote the health of the land and meaningful, deep connection to nature, meaningful ceremonies, and ultimately help us rebuild core systems of human cultures that support connection and care. *Eco-Spirituality in the 21st Century* synthesizes information from a range of traditions and places including ancestral skills, herbalism, bushcraft, permaculture, organic gardening, rewilding, regenerative agriculture, natural building, land regeneration, and more to provide a road map to how we get that better future with joy in our hearts.

In what follows, we have laid out some of the most powerful tools we know from the worlds of magic, permaculture, druidry, eco-spirituality, ancestral skills, herbalism, and nature connection to offer a blueprint for you and your community on how to reweave a better future. Starting in the here and now in your own bioregion, community, and with yourself the healing can begin. *Eco-Spirituality in the 21st Century* offers a powerful vision of the future and the tools to make that happen at a time when we most desperately need it. We offer a vision of a time when humans have repaired and explored a more balanced interaction with the living earth, a vision that offers sacred spirituality rooted in the wisdom of our ancestors, and a vision that creates a world of balance for future generations.

The book is organized into seven chapters, each one a major principle for offering a radical re-envisioning of a new relationship between humanity, nature, and spirit:

- Chapter 1: Reconnection. Reconnecting to the earth, ourselves, and our communities in a deep, meaningful, and lasting way.

- *Chapter 2: Respect.* Developing deep gratitude practices that honor and respect nature.
- *Chapter 3: Rewilding.* Recognizing that we are part of nature, we belong to nature, and working to re-align ourselves with wild spaces, places, and the wilderness within us.
- *Chapter 4: Regeneration.* Recognizing the damage that humans have caused and offering both physical and metaphysical practices for healing that damage; empowering readers to be a force of healing and good.
- *Chapter 5: Resilience.* Cultivating mindsets, practices, and spiritual tools that allow for quick adaptation to a radically changing world.
- *Chapter 6: Reenchantment.* Recognizing the enchantment and magic within nature and the world around us.
- *Chapter 7: ReVisioning.* Recognizing the power of storytelling and visioning in order to create a world where all life can thrive.

The first two chapters serve as a foundation to this work. First we explore how to reconnect with the living earth, ourselves, and our communities, and lay the first stones for a foundation of a better future. Respect explores some of the larger-scale challenges we have faced as human beings and offers tools to put us back into a respectful relationship with the world around us, demonstrating how stable human societies share core features of respectful interaction with nature and the world of spirit. With this foundation, the next three chapters offer three approaches to engaging: rewilding, regeneration, and resilience. These tools show us different ways of living, being, and interacting with our human and nonhuman communities, supporting ecosystems, and exploring our own spirituality and role in the world. Building from the previous five chapters, we reach chapter 6: *Reenchantment*. Reenchanting the world is one of our major goals: developing and cultivating a view of the world that is enchanted, magically responsive, spirit filled, and alive rather than a resource to extract. This world is joyful and connective and helps us right the balance between humans, nature, and spirit. Our final chapter, *ReVisioning*, weaves together the work of the six chapters and offers a clear road map, using visioning and storytelling, to help us bring forth a new paradigm for the future.

Our core six chapters also use a threefold framework: First, we tell stories of past, present, and future—stories of specific places, people, events, or even the earth herself. By sharing the turning point in the present, we weave a brighter future. Second, in addition to the written text, each chapter also features a visual road map and a sigil. The visual road map helps orient the reader to the themes present in the chapter, and the sigils are another magical tool that readers can use for meditation, artwork, and visioning to do this work on both a physical and metaphysical level. We describe the artwork and sigils in more depth in chapter 7: "ReVisioning."

Finally, we adapt the Bard, Ovate, and Druid framework drawn from the teachings of the ancient Druids and modern Druid revival, but rewilded and recrafted for anyone, anywhere. Thus, we use a triple braid of nature, community, and spirit as follows.

OVATE: ***Nature Connection.*** The Ovate theme in each chapter explores our relationship to the natural world around us, including our local ecosystems, local plants and animals, and offers us deep ways of reconnecting to that natural world.

BARD: ***Human and Community Connection.*** The bardic theme explores our relationships with each other in the human realm, which would include building stronger communities, reaching others, and also reaching others with our creative gifts.

DRUID: ***Spirit Connection.*** The Druid theme explores our relationships with the world of spirit, including both our own inner life and spiritual practices as well as exploring core cosmologies that help us build an earth-honoring, nature-reverent future.

Through these three braids, we offer practical skills, tools, meditations, rituals, magical workings, and lore to offer you a road map forward to a brighter future.

Eco-Spirituality in the 21st Century offers a new vision of the future at a time when we most desperately need it. We offer practices that create a brighter vision of the world, a vision in which humans have repaired and explored a more balanced interaction with the living earth, a vision that offers sacred spirituality rooted in the wisdom of our ancestors, and a vision that creates a world of balance for future generations. The ultimate goal of this work is to offer you tools, practices, and vision to unlock your own spiritual and magical potential in becoming a good ancestor and repairing humanity's relationship with nature. Our hope is that this helps us all step up to be the leaders and magicians we need, weaving a new green fire of a brighter future for ourselves and the future generations . . . let us ReVision together!

OVATE
Sit spot practice
baseline ecological
Knowledge
BARD
Storytelling, breaking
bread, building
community
Gaia Hypothesis
DRUID
Creating
Ceremony
tree meditation
Awaken
Realign
Renew
Return
Reconnection

CHAPTER 1

Reconnection

With Nate Summers

Story of the Past:

THE ANCIENT CONNECTION

It is the ancient times, the early times, the dancing times. In the dark, gray early morning during the first hint of dawn, a fire is lit. Five people gather around a fireboard while fire makers sitting in each of the directions take turns spinning a hand drill back and forth. Soon a coal is created and placed in a bundle of thin, light fibers and with the gift of breath fire is born. The flaming tinder bundle is placed in a large stone circle at the center of the village.

As the flames grow and transform the logs of aromatic wood into a burning altar of light and warmth, thirty-three dancers standing in a large circle wrap themselves in deerskin and pull deer skull masks onto their faces. Music is sung, played, chanted, and howled as the dancers become deer.

The deer dancers spin, whirl, and cavort all around the members of the village until the young, the old, the in-between feel the energy of the moment course through their body. The vitality of the red deer surges through everyone causing them to spring up and soon the whole village is dancing.

The energy circulates through the dancers, through the villagers, and then surges out into the land around them and back into the village. Life is nourished, revitalized, and rejuvenated. The villagers and dancers collapse in a heap feeling the sweet exhaustion of dance, life, and ceremony coursing through them.

Connection flows through the people, the land, and the world around them.

INTRODUCING RECONNECTION

One of the strongest and most useful ways to understand human behavior is through the lens and concept of connection. As a species we humans are inherently designed to connect with the world around us. This connection takes many different forms, but ultimately, we are a social species that needs to interact heavily with other humans, with the natural world around us, and arguably with something greater and unseen—Spirit, Mystery or the Divine.

It's common jargon these days to make the claim that we are more connected than ever, especially through the ubiquitous presence of smart phones, social media, and the ever-present internet. Are we really more connected? Or are we pseudo-connected? More and more research is showing that as screen time and social media time increases, depression, anxiety, and other mental health issues increase as well.

Why? What is going on?

Well, consider for a moment what connection has looked like for most of human history. Our primary forms of connection as human beings have consisted of face-to-face interactions with a relatively small (village-sized) group of other human beings on a daily basis. This was combined with daily interaction with a world around us filled with plants, animals, mushrooms, trees, and other beings that we had an intimate relationship with from a very early age.

Rather than living in a time of the greatest connection, we are living in the very opposite: the time of greatest disconnection. We are actually suffering from a crisis of disconnection as our smartphones, computers, technologies, AI, and the Internet create a toxic mimic of real connection that stimulates our brain but leaves it ultimately unsatisfied.

Perhaps an analogy would be helpful. Did you know that white sugar leaches minerals from the body? That's right. Table sugar or white sugar is such a concentrated form of one macronutrient (carbohydrates) that our body literally can't handle it without spiking our insulin and leaching minerals to break it down. Food is supposed to create a feeling of satiety and help us be healthier. White sugar actually does the opposite by making us less healthy and hungrier for actual nutrients.

Now simply consider social media and our smartphones in the same context. We have a longing for real human contact. It's a real, legitimate human need. Instead, we spend time on social media posting and reading and liking content from our "friends"—only a fraction of whom we actually spend time with. We get a temporary spike of dopamine as we like or get liked (similar to the brief spike of energy from sugar), which is followed later (often the next day) by a feeling of depression, emptiness, and craving for another dopamine fix.

What does true connection look like? Feel like? Smell like? What does connection even mean?

Connection is the feeling and sense that we are not completely separate, that we are actually embedded in a series of ***relationships and meaning***. These relationships create a ***sense of security, well-being, and purpose***. Connection is the feeling that a wolf pack has with one another. It's the interweaving of relationships in a forest including plants, trees, and mushroom mycelium. It's also the natural human desire to feel connected to ourselves, nature, community, and spirit. So, what does Reconnection look like or feel like? Well, having been an instructor in skills that help people reconnect for over two decades I can tell you that connection most often smells like food cooking on a fire and people gathered together around that fire at the end of the day . . . let me back up a bit and explain more.

What have we as humans for most of human history actually done? I want you to pause and think about this for a minute. Most people will answer immediately, "Work." But the answer is a lot more nuanced than that, and the true answer is probably different than you think.

The key to the answer is the "most of human history" part of the question. As it is presently understood, humans have been wandering around on this planet in our present form for between at least 60,000 to 200,000 years. That's right, we've been around for that long, and for most of that (190,000 years, according to some), we weren't doing anything remotely like what we consider work nowadays.

Rather than sit in a cubicle all day staring at a screen or being stuck in a factory and literally being an adjunct to a machine, instead humans have spent most of our human history wandering the earth in a natural setting hunting, gathering, and growing our own food and preparing it (and clothes and tools) with other small groups of human beings that we know very, very well. And, then at the end of the day, we would gather around a fire, prepare food, share stories, and make things well into the night. In case you're wondering about the truth of this, consider for a moment that there are actually still groups of people who do this very thing as the basis of their daily existence.

So, what happens when you take a group of modern-day human beings raised in a world very different from this and spend a whole day wandering a natural landscape, gathering wild foods, and then cook and prepare them on a fire?

They lose their minds, in a good way. I can't even describe to you the smiles, the joy, the light in people's faces when they actually get to do something like this. And then later around the fire, people sing, tell stories, laugh, and sometimes openly weep at how amazing it feels to just simply be with other humans outside sharing food.

A little bit different than watching streaming videos, don't you think?

In short, we are facing a disconnection crisis: a disconnection from nature (our original matrix of life), a disconnection from people (our tribe, family, and village), and a disconnection from Spirit (the mysterious, ineffable, and wonderful). One of the key points and purposes of this book is to help provide you the reader with powerful tools to reconnect, to reweave a more hopeful vision for the future, and to help us all tell a better story. How can we Reconnect during these challenging times? And, if we don't, where are we headed as a species and as a planet?

Reconnection as an Ovate

NATURE RECONNECTION

Where does Reconnection start and is it even possible in this day and age? Well, the good news is that we're designed for it. Our human operating system (our brain and being) actually is designed to be connected to nature, other humans, and spirit. While we all probably have individual proclivities and tendencies, a healthy balance of all three is important.

But, during a time of unprecedented ecological crisis and mass overconsumption of resources, I would argue that the best place to start is with Reconnecting with nature and the natural world around us.

For some of us, we may be asking, "But, what does that even look like or feel like?" What a great question, especially the part about "what does it feel like?" One of the simplest, most profound, and best practices of getting people to Reconnect to nature that I've ever seen and experienced is to get people to simply sit still outside in a natural setting and be quiet for at least a little while.

If this sounds a bit like meditating out in nature, it is. But for a lot of people, it's way easier and way more natural than sitting on a cushion indoors in an uncomfortable position. Sit Spot, as it is usually called, is a practice shared by survival schools such as the Tracker School,[5] and made popular by teachers like Jon Young, a deep nature connection specialist, mentor, and visionary who has shared this exercise with thousands of people all over the world.

Sounds too easy? Sounds like it is something really, ancient, old, and like a precursor to meditation? Both might actually be right. Gary Snyder, beat poet, ecological advocate, and Zen practitioner has suggested repeatedly that our indoor sitting meditation practices originated from hunters who used to sit still in nature for long periods of time. The inherent quiet and stillness that arises in our brains during these experiences may actually be a key part of human neurobiology that allowed us to be successful hunters and gatherers and also helped us survive by avoiding being found by predators as well.

Sit Spot practice

How do you even start doing a Sit Spot practice? It's surprisingly straightforward, simple, and wonderful. To start with you just need to find a spot in nature that you can go and sit and be relatively undisturbed by people for at least fifteen minutes. The more undisturbed nature the better, but that being said, I know people that have used their backyards as their Sit Spot for decades and I've had Sit Spots in urban parks numerous times. If you can, find a tree to sit against and have a landscape in front of you that is relatively open and free of human interference. Creeks, ponds, rivers, hills, forests, deserts, and even mountains are great, but you don't need to go to the wilderness to make this happen.

So, find your spot, go there, and then just sit . . . no, really, it's that simple. It can be helpful to gently tune into your senses one by one when you get there, and if you get distracted simply come back to your senses. This may be a little bit hard at first, but it will get easier with practice. No devices, no podcasts, just quiet time in nature by sitting still by yourself without talking—probably the oldest most natural form of meditation in the world.

If you can go every day, that is best. But several times a week will work. Dawn and dusk are ideal times for seeing wildlife and for more quietness from other humans. Doing this regularly becomes one of the best and deepest ways to connect to nature around you. Having a Sit Spot less than ten minutes from your house is best, and you should find what works for you.

Baseline Ecological Knowledge

While Sit Spot is a great start and a foundational way to connect to nature, there are of course a myriad of other ways including hiking, camping, wildcrafting or foraging, outdoor recreation like rock climbing or kayaking—the list is endless. Everyone may have their own path and way with this. However, there is another core way of reconnecting to nature that we should all consider.

While it's difficult to realize, once upon a time *all humans* lived in such a way that they hunted, gathered, and made everything they needed from their local environment. There were no grocery stores. There were no big box stores delivering everything after a click of a button. While this may sound like a nightmare to some, humans were completely capable of living sustainably and regeneratively with the land and nature around them. How is this even possible?

Well, in those times all human beings grew up immersed and enmeshed in a web of learning and traditional knowledge that provided a solid baseline **ecological knowledge** of the world around them. This included knowing all of the local plants, fungi, and trees, the local animal life including mammals, reptiles and amphibians, birds, insects and other arthropods. But more than just knowing the names of things or what they looked like, people had a *relationship* with all of these beings. They also knew how to harvest, use, and work with all the natural world around them.

Can you imagine what it would be like to have all your needs taken care of by the world around you? What would it be like to hand-harvest and hand-make your food, clothes, shelter, medicine, and everything else? What would the world be like if we all had a baseline ecological knowledge of our place and one that could grow into a more broad and robust Traditional ecological knowledge of where we live? And how can we possibly hope to rediscover this kind of knowledge, awareness, and connection? Having these kinds of relationships are one form of decolonizing our consciousness and being while also reindigenizing our relationship with nature and the world around us.

While it may seem quite daunting and overwhelming, we can start simply by getting to know our neighbors: the nonhuman ones. We live in a time of unprecedented access to knowledge and information through portable devices most of us carry most of the time. In those devices are names and information about all of the trees, plants, fungi, birds, mammals, insects, and other nonhuman beings that live all around you. These names and identities are just the start of beginning to build your baseline ecological knowledge. Book knowledge and online sources can only take us so far and really are just a supportive part of the process. They can often be the beginning of a relationship. What is baseline ecological knowledge? While it's a modern term that has grown in use in the last twenty years, the idea it represents is much older. Simply put, baseline ecological knowledge is the understanding, knowledge, wisdom, and connection everyone should naturally have with the ecosystem they live in. Here are some examples of baseline ecological knowledge.

- Knowing what trees in your area make good firewood

- Knowing the edible plants in your bioregion for each season of the year
- Knowing the major predators of your area, their tracks and signs, and how to have a healthy relationship with them
- Knowing which birds stay year-round in your area and which birds leave in migration and why

This is just scratching the surface, but notice that the list of things we could know as part of our baseline ecological knowledge are inherently connective, require observation and relationship, and are not necessarily things we can simply look up in a book. Here is a list of practices to consider undertaking that reflect some of the key concepts above.

- Exploring deeply the ethnobotany (the Indigenous use of plants and trees for medicine, food, and technology) of your region. This includes learning to ethically and carefully harvest plant foods and medicine, as well as learning other forms of plant technology such as fire making, cordage making, or fiber arts.
- Learning the common tracks, signs, appearance, and behavior of the top ten major mammals in your bioregion, especially for any large or dangerous mammals including predators.
- Finding out what are the major hazards of your area, including weather, animals, plants, climate, and others.
- Taking up the practice of birdwatching and in addition studying and learning about bird vocalizations, language, and behavior and how they can tell you about what's happening in the natural world around you.
- Studying the flow of water in your landscape. Where does it come from and where does it go to? How does it change over time? How healthy are your water sources in the region?
- Learning and developing a relationship with the trees of your bioregion, including ethnobotany, folklore, and practical

knowledge of tree ecology. How are the trees doing where you live? How are they responding to climate change?

- Discover the insects, fish, amphibians, and reptiles of your bioregion. Where do they live? What do they do through seasonal changes? How could you catch them if you wanted?
- Take up the practice of foraging for mushrooms. Learn to safely identify and harvest them and undersatand what role they play in the ecosystem.

Where might you learn some of this knowledge, especially if so much of it has been lost in modern times? Throughout the globe, people are relearning and committing to these practices through communities in the earth skills and ancestral skills movements. Thus, you might see if there is a local event or gathering, or a school teaching bushcraft, ancestral skills, earth skills, and so forth. Many of these places can connect you with teachers and a broader community exploring how to build, reestablish, and maintain deep connections to the local land.

To set yourself on the journey toward baseline ecological knowledge that can grow and grow, I encourage you to start by learning five local trees, five local edible plants, five local medicinal plants, five local mammals, five insects, five local birds, five fungi, and five reptiles and amphibians, then journal, write, or draw a bit about each including how they relate to each other, to humans and our needs, and how they fit into the bigger picture.

Are you connected to your human neighbors? Are there some of them whose names you don't know? Are there some whose names you know, but little else? How about some neighbors that you chitchat with or are friends with? I believe it's the same with our ecological neighbors as well. While it can be a good start to know the names of the local flora and fauna around us, that's just the beginning of how to develop baseline ecological knowledge.

I'll give you an example: many folks have been on a nature walk or plant walk with a naturalist or ranger where the leader of the hike simply names plants or animals or trees for everybody along the hike. At the end of the little excursion, most people only remember a name or two. But, if the same naturalist tells a story or two about a specific plant or animal, or they have people reach out and touch and smell trees and plants along the walk, people are way more likely to remember what they learned.

It's the same on our journey with baseline ecological knowledge. If we learn stories, lore, information, and have experiences with our ecological neighbors, we are way more likely to remember and feel connected to them.

So, which five trees, plants, mammals, birds, etc., should you start with? Go ask your Sit Spot. No, really, that's the place to start. After all, those are the neighbors you will be spending the most time with. Don't be afraid to grab local field guides from your library, and use online resources to start growing your relationships with your neighbors. If you really want to challenge yourself, see what kind of local Indigenous language and knowledge there is available around your neighbors as well. *Make sure that your relationship includes aspects of observation and direct interaction, not just knowledge acquired from reading about species.*

And don't be surprised if after you've connected with those basic five species of each of those core areas, you want to go deeper and deeper learning more and more about the species around you as you grow your web of friendship, connection, and relationship.

Connecting to Nature for Your Basic Needs

These two practices, Sit Spot and developing baseline ecological knowledge, are a potent one–two combination mutually feeding and nourishing each other. And, they form a foundation for deeper connection to nature that can happen over time and in a variety of ways. However, a third way of reconnecting to nature that leaps out at us when we look at ancestral ways and primary ways is finding a way to have our basic needs met from the natural world, in at least small ways. Again, this can be the start or deepening the process of reindigenizing our relationship with the world around us. What do I mean here? Well, let's pause for a moment and consider water. Did you know that once upon a time, the only form of water that people consumed was wild, natural water from springs, streams, rivers, and lakes? Did you know that there was a very, very long period of time where you could drink safely and easily from most natural sources of water? Can you imagine the freedom, flow, and fun of drinking wild water after a day of hiking or as the first thirst-quenching drink after a night of camping? These kinds of primary experiences are not as far away as we might imagine. Getting people to have their basic needs of shelter, warmth, water, and food met from the natural world is one of the most empowering, enlightening, and invigorating things I've ever had the opportunity to teach. People become truly alive after making a fire from materials gathered from the land around them, from foraging wild berries or greens, or from sleeping in a natural shelter they build themselves.

Of course, things are different now, and it's a rare opportunity that we can drink from a safe source of wild water (though researching natural springs in your area is a good start), we can purify wild water, forage berries, nuts, and greens safely and respectfully, make fire with wood we gather ourselves, and build shelters to sleep under while our bodies are nestled in the earth's embrace.

Here's a sample list of some fun, easy, and creative ways to reconnect to nature through meeting your basic needs.

- Filter wild water from a wild source and drink it fresh.
- Take a foraging class in your own area and safely learn to gather small amounts of food from the landscape.
- Learn to safely make fires using tinder, kindling, and fuel gathered from the land. Up-level your skills by learning to make a friction fire (a big challenge but super satisfying).
- Take a survival skills course or ancestral living skills course from a school near you.
- Sleep under a shelter you build from natural materials.
- Sleep under the stars next to a fire that you and a friend tend all night.
- Learn about gathering and making medicine from the plants and trees of your bioregion.
- Take a mycology course and learn about the power of fungi for foraging and medicine.

The list is incomplete, of course, and this is just the beginning. However, learning to do these things combined with Sit Spot and developing true relationships with the species around you is an incredibly powerful and solid set of practices that will form deep reconnection to nature. It's also a never-ending journey, and it's quite possible through these practices you will develop a deeper understanding of and a deeper feeling of what it means to be *truly human.*

If you are wondering how to get started on this journey or are feeling a little overwhelmed, realize that there is now a decades-old, worldwide movement devoted to helping with these reconnection skills and practices. For example, Rabbitstick Rendezvous was started over thirty years ago in northern Idaho as a place for people to gather and share survival skills, ancestral skills, and go deep in reconnection. The annual gathering was so popular that it soon added a winter gathering in northern Arizona known as Wintercount.[6] Now, ancestral and survival skills gatherings take place all over North America and all over the world with gatherings happening almost every calendar month. This coupled with the explosion of survival and deep nature connection schools all over the world makes it easier than ever to find a community of like-minded people going on a similar journey.

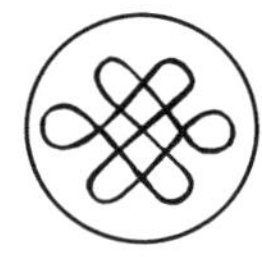

Story of the Present:

LEARNING TO RECONNECT

A series of thirty-three enigmatic deer-skull masks are discovered at the famous Star Carr archeological site in northeastern England. The masks are estimated to be at least 11,000 years old and are part of one of the largest Mesolithic sites in the United Kingdom filled with all sorts of artifacts including beaded necklaces, antler tools, pendants, stone tools, and more. The latest understanding of the masks is that they were most likely used for ceremonial purposes and the large number of masks found at the village suggest a huge cultural importance.

Meanwhile, during unprecedented times including massive global climate change, intense political instability, and economic challenges people seek connection. Often they turn to their portable electronic devices seeking likes and comments from their "friends" from all over the globe. Simultaneously, around the globe other forms of reconnection are growing and swirling in an organic mix. Ancestral skills gatherings where people learn to make stone tools, fire, and natural clothes and fibers have taken off all over the world. Survival and deep nature connection schools that teach both youth and adults are popping up all over. Permaculture trainings and workshops that teach people how to reconnect with their own backyard turning them into food forests, plant and animal sanctuaries, and herbal medicine spiral gardens happen with more and more frequency. At the same time, there is a worldwide explosion of interest in earth-based spiritual traditions including Druidry, Neo-Paganism, and Gaia worship.

Schools, movements, nongovernmental organizations, and a plethora of grassroots movements are laying the foundation to reconnect people to each other, to nature, and to the mysteries of spirit.

Reconnection as a Bard

REWEAVING PEOPLE AND COMMUNITY

To be honest the idea of being a wilderness hermit definitely has an appeal to me, as I'm sure it does to many of you. However, time has shown that people do need people, and in fact, human connection or people connection is another aspect of reconnection that is just as important as nature connection. We are social animals, after all.

There was definitely a time in my life when I was at the point where I really felt that nature was "good" and people were "bad." My views have changed quite a bit, and I like to think that my views have become a bit more nuanced including the realization that humans are nature as well. When I was younger, I did idealize living in nature by myself, but after having practiced multiple solo survival trips, it became clear: We need each other.

To illustrate this further, I'd like to share with you the myth of the happy, solitary mountain man. This is the idea that for some period of time in the 1700s and 1800s that there were a plethora of mountain men living wild, fun, carefree, adventurous lives in the American West, especially in the Rocky Mountains. Like most myths and stories there is a kernel of truth: There were a number of men living in the mountains who hunted and trapped for fur and lived remotely from villages and other people. They probably had pretty extensive knowledge and awareness to live in intense wilderness situations and conditions. However, they were completely dependent on nearby towns for trading their goods (mostly furs) in exchange for food, tools, and other things they couldn't make themselves. While that existence might have appealed to some, especially younger folks, there's a big secret nobody shares . . . almost all of the mountain men died young. That's right, the average age of death was right around forty years of age. The existence of living most of your life isolated from others, trying to do it all yourself, and only periodically coming into town to trade took a heavy toll on people.

Does this mean it doesn't work for some? No. But it's clear from the anthropological literature that most people living throughout most of human history have lived embedded in a group of people—a village or tribe, and being kicked out of that group was considered one of the greatest forms of punishment available.

We long for, thrive with, and need people connection.

But in the days and age of screentime, social media, and constant news, how can we reestablish good connections with people? There's definitely a need for real, in-person connection for all of us.

The pandemic and its aftermath certainly hasn't made anything easier for most of us. But it is important to remember that at our core part of being human is connecting with others. One of the things that can make connecting with people challenging in our current world is that the number of people we interface with on a daily and weekly basis may be vastly different than what our brains expect. We can be exposed to way more people than we expect or way less.

Just imagine for a moment growing up in a small village of between forty to sixty people with a decent number of the people around being people you are somehow related to. If you want, imagine that on a daily basis you work with these people on projects outside either growing, hunting, or gathering food, making medicine, or making some form of handicraft. Perhaps within the edge of walking distance of a half day there is another village of a similar number of people. This is your village, your tribe, your band, and there are others around that sometime you gather with or meet with or even have conflict with. Now, imagine that this is how *it has been your whole life.*

This might sound dreadful to some people and overwhelming to a lot of folks, but it's important to note that something like the above is how most people lived in prehistoric times and some people around the world still live this way today. A few leading psychologists are basically putting forth the idea that our brains are designed for way fewer people in our lives and that those connections were way more intimate and familiar than what we experience now. So, how do we go about building such a band or tribe? While there are many ways to do this, three core practices stick out:

- Pursuing a common interest with others outside (gardening, hiking, camping, food preservation, natural crafts)
- Joining together with others in preparing and/or the eating of a meal at a regular time and place, ideally outdoors
- Having a group of folks to share your nature and outdoor stories with and being an active listener and contributor with this group.

Common Interest Nature Groups

Finding common interests outdoors is a great beginning. This can be a hiking, kayaking, rock climbing, naturalist, mushrooming or wildcrafting club or group. In fact, I'm not sure that the specific activity matters as much as that it is done outside, together and consistently, ideally once a month or more. Having a common group pursuing a common interest outside is a fundamental way to reconnect with others, and it can form a solid basis for human connection.

Here it's also probably good to think outside the box. What about joining or starting a gardening or permaculture club? How about a group of home brewers? Or, a group of natural builders working with local materials and building cob benches, earth ovens, and other outdoor-based natural buildings? The possibilities are endless. A few years ago, an older gentleman shared with me on a trip his love of smoking meats over a fire in his backyard. This passion and love he shared with a close group of family and friends, and it became a weekly ritual that brought together everybody outside around a fire all day. Another great example from the Midwest and Northeast of the United States is how people gather together around the practice of maple sugaring: multiple days of boiling sap down over a fire, outside, in groups of people. An ancient and modern practice rolled up all together.

Sharing Food Together Outside

These last two examples clearly start to bring together both our number one and number two options: pursuing a common interest together outdoors and including food as part of it. The joy of sharing a meal outdoors with others is one of the oldest human traditions, and frankly often served as a way of showing and making peace between differing groups of people. A few years ago when I was leading daylong nature excursions for people from all over the world to both Mount Rainier National Park and Olympic National Park, one of the key moments on the trip for the group of ten to twelve strangers was when we had a midday meal outside. Everyone would smile, lighten up, and it's as if our group congealed and a group identity was born. This group identity would carry on into the afternoon with a general feeling of lightness and wonder as we explored the majesty of the national parks, however one of everybody's favorite moments was actually the delicious meal shared outdoors together. Heck, even on the days it rained, people still enjoyed the picnic together in a beautiful setting as we all changed from being strangers to being friends, if only for a day.

Sharing Our Stories in Person

The next piece that can be woven in is the telling of stories. While there is a long, healthy tradition worldwide of talented storytellers getting up and sharing epic stories of places and people long ago, there is also the more humble storytelling tradition of simply sharing your own story with a group of attentive listeners. Both of these traditions and all of the variations of storytelling on the spectrum inbetween have a valued spot in reconnection practices. In fact, if you think deeply about it the popularity of Facebook, Instagram, and TikTok is really all about people sharing their stories. In the face of the growing use of AI to construct and design content, the originality of sharing our own story with other real life humans becomes not only novel, but powerful and even revolutionary.

Imagine gathering around a fire outside at night, underneath the stars. Slowly people began to share with the group the stories of their adventures from the day. Highlights are shared as well as challenges, triumphs and tragedies. There is laughter, giggles, gasps, and perhaps even a few tears. After a bit, someone breaks into song, and everyone slowly joins in. Finally, an elder stands before the gathering and shares a story of long ago, of the people, of the land, and of connection. Everyone's imagination is lit up, the story plays out in the mind's eye of everyone present, and at the end there is a quiet deep, sweet silence. Slowly, everyone moves off to their sleeping areas, their souls and spirits fed by the stories of everyone around them.

How powerful are stories? Well, it's pretty clearly been determined that they are one of the best ways we learn as human beings, and it might be that they are the ***most powerful way of conveying a message***.

Just ask the advertising industry or any social media group . . . they are basically all forms of storytelling. In fact, you might have noticed that storytelling is a key component of the premise of this book. What you are holding in your hands and reading is an attempt to tell a better, more powerful story of the world we can all live in.

These three again work best in concert, forming another triad of powerful connection. Imagine joining a group of friends outside for a day of wandering, playing, and foraging together. Then you gather in the late afternoon preparing a meal together in an outdoor kitchen. Amidst the scent of woodsmoke and the flickering of fire you cook the meal together on an outdoor fire and in an earthen oven. After sharing the delicious, savory flavors of your foraged meal, you gather around the fire to share songs, stories, and favorite moments from the landscapes and places of the day. Reconnection happens all around.

Reconnection as a Druid

SPIRIT RECONNECTION

While it may be relatively easy to find ways to reconnect with people and nature, the idea of reconnecting spiritually is a whole other challenge. Another way of framing this book is really about helping us all find our own spirit reconnection through an ecological lens and focus. But spirituality and belief varies greatly from person to person, especially in this day and age. When we approach reconnecting to Spirit, rather than offering specific concrete dogmatic ideas, concepts, or scripture, instead we have chosen to offer a series of practices, stories, and ways of being that help "point the way" to the spiritual, which will probably look and feel a bit different for each of us.

A core staple of most forms of spirituality is some method of quieting the mind and loosening the identity or ego so that a sense of stillness and oneness permeates one's being. These kinds of practices are usually called meditations of some sort, though that term may not actually be useful or accurate either. The Sit Spot mentioned earlier in this chapter is a really powerful, natural, and ancient form of meditation.

While it has become quite common around the world for people to practice a form of sitting meditation, it is much less common (especially in the present North America) for people to practice forms of standing meditation. With our exceedingly sedentary culture, which involves a ton of sitting, a standing meditation practice can be of great benefit to one's mind and body, especially one that takes place outdoors and involves nature imagery.

Tree Meditation Practice

The following practice is known as Standing Like a Tree, Embracing the Tree, or Big Tree Meditation. Different versions of the exercise are practiced in East Asian energetic arts, as well as some versions practiced in modern neo-Pagan and eco-spirituality groups.

This exercise is best done outside. Stand in a comfortable position with the feet about hip width apart. The feet can turn out slightly or be straight forward. Imagine that the crown of the head is relaxed upward toward the sky and is gently lifted up by a string. Allow the major joints of the body including the shoulders, elbows, wrists, hips, knees, and ankles to relax and bend slightly. Allow the sacrum and tailbone to relax and soften long, and imagine you are about to sit down on a high stool (this should allow the sacrum and tailbone to relax even more).

Let your awareness sink down into your feet and then deeper into the earth. Feel your feet and lower body rooted to the earth. Next, gently let the hands float up to just below the navel. The hands will face your body with the fingers gently spread apart. It's as if your hands are wrapped around the trunk of a tree just in front of you with the palms facing toward your navel and lower abdomen. Look for a feeling of softness, roundness, and fullness and feel free to adjust how close or how far away your hands are until you are comfortable.

Next, visualize in your mind's eye that you are a tree. Feel your roots connected down to the earth. Let the trunk of your body be the trunk of the tree. Feel your trunk extend up into the sky through your head and feel your branches spreading all around. Pick any kind of tree or a very specific tree that you have an affinity with to become.

Spend several minutes just being a tree with your awareness gently resting below your navel. Feel your roots, sense your branches, feel your crown extending into the heavens. Become the tree.

When you are ready to finish gently allow your hands to come back to the body and rest on the navel. Let the image of the tree slowly dissolve and disappear. Then lightly massage the body from head to toe, and if it feels good gently shake or vibrate the body before walking around. Contemplate what it feels like to be a tree.

Cosmology: The Gaia Hypothesis

Another key part of many different spiritual paths is cosmology, or an understanding of how the world is and came to be. Many of us carry big wounds around cosmology because we may have grown up with cosmology that was pretty dogmatic. This can include the dogma of scientific materialism, which is a belief that nothing has spirit at all and that we are simply the result of chemistry and physics playing itself out. An argument could be made that dogmatic scientific materialism is actually one of the biggest causes of disconnection around.

Regardless, any spiritual path that is attempting to reconnect us to the mysterious, the numinous, and Spirit itself needs to have some cosmology to it. In this book, we are providing multiple cosmological keys, maps, and concepts and the advice is to go with what resonates and feels best to you and your path.

Any attempt at having a healthy eco-spirituality with reconnection as a focus can simply turn to one of the oldest archetypal images and cosmological ideas of all time: Mother Earth. Found in almost every world religion and spiritual tradition, the personification of the Earth as a feminine nurturing force is a key to reconnecting with nature, community, and spirit. Whether it's Gaia from the Greeks, Danu from Ireland, Pachamama from South and Central America, the idea of Mother Nature from folk traditions, or the countless other variations, when we honor and treat the earth as alive and worthy of respect and veneration, reconnection to the original spirit begins.

Seeing the Earth as a sacred, divine, spiritual being worthy of respect doesn't necessarily imply worship, but it certainly heavily suggests veneration. While this may seem like a very spiritual and nonmaterialist approach, there is also a strong scientific basis behind these ideas as well. In the late '70s and early '80s, the Gaia Hypothesis was put forth by James Lovelock.[7] Taking the traditional Greek name for the divine female Earth goddess, Lovelock suggested that our world itself is alive and actually functions like one giant organism. Human beings are merely one of many, many different species that are part of a much larger symbiotic organism in the form of our planet, known as Earth.

What does all of this mean? How does it inform an eco-spiritual path? Rather than providing answers, perhaps it is better to ask questions that open and reveal instead:

- What is your relationship to the Earth?
- Do you feel a spiritual connection to the Earth?
- What strengthens or weakens this connection?
- What are ways you nourish the Earth in your life?
- If you were to regard the Earth as some form of sentient being, what would that feel like?
- What is your relationship with your mother and your grandmothers?
- Do you see any parallels with your relationship with the Earth?
- How does your relationship with the Earth change if you consider it a living, feminine being worthy of reverence, respect, and ceremony?
- What kind of ceremony would you do to honor, nourish, and strengthen the Earth?

Creating Ceremony

When we talk about ceremony, we are talking about the human need to step away from the mundane world and connect with something deeper than ourselves, to take a moment to honor and acknowledge the world around you, and to raise or work with energy for healing, blessing, and abundance in the world. Ceremonies are as old as people and bringing them back into our daily rhythms and lives is a way for us to reconnect with the earth, our spirits, and weave our communities back together.

As humans we also have a deep inherent longing and need for ceremony. In particular, I have seen that humans have the need for powerful, collective experience that connects them to something much larger than themselves: the ineffable, the mysterious, the numinous. Taking on the practice of recreating ceremony both for ourselves, our community, and the world around us can be a daunting task. It might also be a lifetime's worth of work.

However, there are also lots of simple ways to start rebuilding and reweaving ceremonies of reconnection for us and others. Here are some simple, yet powerful building blocks of connective ceremony:

- Build a fire by yourself or with others. Offer something to the fire as a form of thanks or gratitude (ideally something burnable). Traditional offerings include food, oil, aromatic herbs you gathered yourself, tree resin incense you gathered yourself, tobacco, or something beautiful you made. Alternatively, use the fire as a catalyst for a letting go ceremony.

- Either with a group of people or by yourself gather near a source of freshwater that is part of your local bioregion (river, lake, stream, creek, or spring). Sing to the waters as an offering. Visualize the waters being clean, purified, and healthy now and in the future.

- Gather with others in the forest in a natural clearing or space. Offer gratitude to the trees and the land around you and then have one of you play a drum or another musical instrument. Dance as a sacred offering and blessing to the animals around you. Become the animals as you visualize yourself shapeshifting. Dance your prayers, dance your blessing, dance your animal into being.

- When you come across a place of natural beauty, take a ceremonial moment. Be present in that place, make offerings, sing, dance, and simply honor being present in this space.

Ceremonies do not have to be formal, scripted, or even created in advance. They can be intuitive, joyful, and free. Finding ways to build ceremony into your life is a powerful, moving method of reconnection. The above practices are just the beginning of how we explore ceremonies in this book, but even the simplest ceremonies are meaningful, joyful, and ultimately connecting. We explore some more specific steps to creating ceremonies, in chapter 3: "Rewilding."

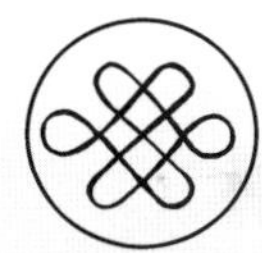

Story of the Future:

CONNECTION EMBRACED

The reconnection movement has spread everywhere. People gather regularly with each other, outdoors, and honor the natural world realizing this is ultimately what it means to be human. Masks are created for the animals, the trees, the birds, the fungi, for all beings. Fires are lit, illuminating the young, the old, and everyone inbetween. Music is played on handmade instruments beneath the full moon and the starry firmament.

People don their costumes and masks and are transformed in the flickering firelight. A dance begins . . . a dance as old as time. As the dance spirals out, the earth is rejuvenated and renewed. The deer herds swell, the wolf packs howl, the salmon proliferate, the fungi glow and flicker with messages, light, and intelligence rejuvenating the forests. Life is nourished, and the Great Mother smiles gently at her children.

RESPECT
DRUID
Animism
Being a Custodian of the Land
Opening Heartspaces
BARD
Gratitude in Community & in Foodways
Hospitality Traditions
OVATE
Deep gratitude
Reciprocation with Nature
Offerings

CHAPTER 2

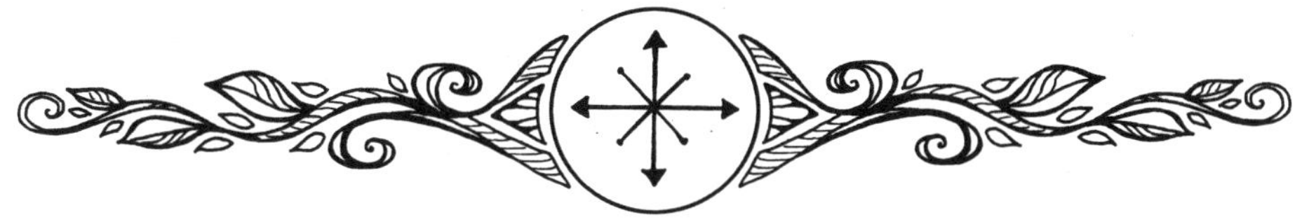

Respect

With Dana O'Driscoll

Story of the Past:

ONE HISTORY OF THE WORLD

On the lands of what was and is still sometimes known as Turtle Island, a variety of different cultures and peoples lived in relative harmony with nature. Contrary to some present beliefs, they had very advanced cultures with deep senses of history, storytelling, equity, and social structures. For example, in what is now known as Poverty Point in Louisiana, ancient Indigenous peoples of the Americas gathered to practice ceremonies, trade, and exchange stories. Thousands of people, traveling from as far as 800 miles away, would gather at this rich cultural center. Farther north, the tribes of the Eastern Woodlands, including the Iroquois, Ojibwe, Shawnee, and Lenape, had extremely egalitarian cultures and were adept in skilled crafts, agriculture, hunting and fishing, and herbal medicine. These rich, ancient cultures tended the land, created extremely advanced systems of agriculture, and lived in harmonious, balanced interaction with nature. On the other side of the Atlantic, a similar story was once present. Traditional Indigenous and pagan European cultures thrived, connected to nature and honoring a variety of nature-centric deities, festivals, and traditions.

One of the first forms of colonization, the spread of Christianity, took place during the third through ninth centuries, displacing both traditional relationships with the land and traditional lifeways. At the same time, Islam was colonizing the traditional Indigenous beliefs of much of Africa, the Middle East, and parts of Asia. These conversions from diverse, Indigenous religions to monotheism were fundamental to later waves of colonialism that spread throughout the world.

Rooted in attitudes of dominion and empire, Europeans undermined their natural resource base. Along with resource depletion, Europeans increasingly depended on trade routes to Asia, which brought precious metals, silk, and spices, as well as cultural knowledge. In the 1400s, these routes were disrupted by the Ottoman Empire, and Europeans began looking for another way to trade and get their necessary resources from Asia. After Columbus landed in the Caribbean in 1492, England, Spain, France, and the Netherlands began to send explorers and colonists to explore, exploit, and profit from what became known as the New World. This led not only to the enslavement, genocide, and colonization of the Indigenous peoples who lived in the Americas but also to the exploitation and destruction of the ecosystem—that had been so carefully tended by those caretaking peoples for millennia.

The human costs of colonialization are horrific and involve often the complete eradication or subjugation of people or the erasure of entire ways of life. But what isn't as well known is that colonialism also enacts terrible costs ecologically. As John Richards[8] *explores, four broad historical processes from 1500 to 1800 shaped the land during colonization: biological invasion (where non-native species were brought without consideration of their impact on the ecosystem), commercial hunting of wildlife, destructive human land use that depletes the land, and energy scarcity. Both of these colonial processes—the forced displacement of people and ecological destruction—form the tapestry of the entire globe that we live on today. Thus, this past story is hardly unique to North America—Indigenous peoples throughout the globe, including in Asia, Africa, South America, and Australia likewise had sustaining, nature-connected cultures.*

Although Europe represents only 8% of the landmass of Earth, Europeans colonized or conquered more than 80% of the world,[9] *with only five present-day countries escaping some form of this colonial legacy. In fact, the colonial worldview and attitudes are now perpetuated everywhere by peoples of all colors and have become an invisible foundation of our modern world.*

INTRODUCING RESPECT

At the heart of the schisms that happened between humans and nature and at the heart of the story I just told above is the principle of Respect: engaging in respectful interaction, respecting the sovereignty of other beings, and respecting the sovereignty of nature. *Merriam Webster's* dictionary[10] defines Respect in several important ways for our purposes. As a noun, Respect includes "an act of giving particular attention" (consideration); "high or special regard or deference" (esteem); the quality or state of being" (esteemed). As a verb, Respect is important in the context of our work today; we can hold respect in our minds and hearts. We can also engage in respectful actions—and both of these are necessary for our purposes.

As our opening story shares, colonial mindsets represent the antithesis of respect—these behaviors do not respect the living earth, the peoples that inhabit those places, or their sovereignty. Colonizers exhibit a narcissism that implies that people and land are better off under their control. Colonization at its roots includes a lack of respect for the sovereignty of other cultures and a lack of respect for the sovereignty of life on this planet.

Despite much recent criticism of the historical past, these colonial attitudes continue to prevail because they are foundational to Western and now global culture. Colonial beliefs continue to fuel modern Western civilization, through its emphasis on greed, a hunger that is never sated, consumption, materialism, and commitment to growth at all costs. Colonialism has evolved from settler colonialism with the domination of land and culture to the present form of economic domination where rich countries extract the human and natural resources of poorer ones. In *Braiding Sweetgrass*, Robin Wall Kimmerer offers the Anishinaabe description of the Windigo to describe colonialism. Windigo is the beast that consumes everything in its path without any self-control—and she argues that the spirit of the Windigo and its footprints are the goal of modern economics, felt from the strip mines to corporate boardrooms of our modern age.

I think there is power in framing this current age as a form of collective insanity in which greed and overconsumption have become the driving forces of the world. I could fill a book with examples, but I'll limit them to just a few compelling ones. First, despite ample evidence of human-driven climate change—so much that we are now in the age of the Anthropocene, the age of global-scale human change on Earth—we continue to emit more and more pollutants and continue to resist the necessary major cultural and life shifts necessary to stop climate change. We are seeing the results of climate change in increasing ways all over the globe, and yet, these larger economic and colonial systems resist stopping it. In addition to climate change, we have a sixth mass extinction happening, where literally all life is threatened and dying, and it doesn't even make the news. And while many people individually are doing everything they can to reduce their own footprint, human civilization is hell-bent on continuing to privilege greed, growth at all costs, and consuming and destroying the planet. It is hard to step back from this present age of insanity and fathom why enormous, broader, and far-reaching changes are not taking place.

The impact of living in such an age, and being surrounded by the insanity that is normalized is taking its toll on all life. On the human side, symptoms include declining mental and physical health; increased violence, shootings, and political instability; and an eroding of our basic foundations of community and relationships with each other. On the side of all other life, the cost is that life itself and the future of our planet. That's why we are writing this book—to help us move out of the colonial legacy and collective insanity present in the world and into a place of Earth-honoring living and being in the world. To re-indigenize where we are, to learn to hear the spirits of nature once again and put humans back into a caring relationship with nature. And as the opening story and these last few paragraphs have described, we are talking about undoing centuries of problematic human thinking, which is ongoing—and yet necessary work—if we are to survive and protect life on this planet.

Obviously, the problems above are clear—and to address these, we continue our work understanding the principle of respect. Respect is one of the most fundamental practices for the work of undoing colonization and stepping away from the present collective insanity. Because colonialism has been a driving force on this planet for five centuries, much of our own cultural baggage involves recognizing these historical and present systems and working to end them. The heart of the challenge we face in transitioning from a life-destroying culture to a life-honoring one is in respect. Specifically, it is to disentangle the many underlying myths and narratives that subconsciously or consciously drive our behaviors and that thereby impact our interactions with other life on this planet.

As heavy as the problems and above are, the work of respect is simple, easy to learn, and straightforward. For our purposes, *respect* has the following features:

- Having a deep admiration and high opinion of all beings in nature and nature herself
- Acknowledging the sovereignty of all beings (their right to self-determination)

- Honoring the living earth and all living beings with practices of gratitude and seeking permission
- Developing sets of reciprocal practices where we both give and take from the living earth

While we can apply respect to everything on the earth: the blades of grass, the mountains, the rivers, the flock of geese, the cabbage in our garden—we can also apply respect to our fellow human beings. By bringing respect back into our daily lives, our daily conversations, and our approach to interacting with all beings, we can begin to undo these historical legacies that have shaped the world and build something new, something better, something that is sustaining and life affirming. And by doing that, we rebuild the reciprocal connections between humans and the earth on an individual, community, and global level. So, for the rest of this chapter, we delve into the work of respect.

Respect as an Ovate

GRATITUDE, OFFERINGS, AND RECIPROCATION

As we've explored above, a major issue we have at present in the world is a lack of respect for nature and all living beings. We began to build respectful interactions through Ovate reconnection practices; practices such as Sit Spot and establishing Baseline Ecological Knowledge begin the long process of reorienting ourselves to the living earth.

Deep Gratitude

One of the problems with industrialization, consumption, and materialism is that we lack a true sense of gratitude for the earth that provides for us. The system purposely disconnects us from our food and the sources of our food and the land that sustains us. The system masks the sources of nature which provide the goods we use (e.g., the "distributed by" label) or the hands that make those goods. Instead of having gratitude for nature, which literally provides our every need, we have brand loyalty. Companies and corporations steal that loyalty, cultivate it, and we somehow feel beholden to them rather than the living earth. But the true source of our clothing, housing, food, and possessions is the earth. One way to reorient ourselves in a respectful way is by practicing deep gratitude. If gratitude is taking a moment to say thank you, deep gratitude takes that a bit further. Deep gratitude is a practice and a mindset. It includes the following:

- Taking small moments to acknowledge what nature has provided to you and be in gratitude for those gifts.
- Acknowledging the natural resources, lives, and offerings from nature that have been given so that you can thrive.
- Acknowledging the hands and labor that have grown, harvested, produced, moved, and sold things to you so that you can be healthy, comfortable, and well fed.
- Being grateful for all things, human-made or natural, and sharing that gratitude freely.
- Slowing down enough to be grateful for what you have and how it has come to you.

The practice itself is simple. If you are consuming anything, take a moment for gratitude. If you eat something, have gratitude. If you purchase something, have gratitude. You want to honor the life or resources that were given, because something is almost always used when we consume. If you are somewhere, thank the materials of the building, which was provided by the earth. Take a moment to simply express your gratitude and thanks for what nature has provided you.

For example, let's say you are having a banana for breakfast that you bought at the grocery store. Before you eat, take a moment for gratitude. First, offer gratitude to the tree that that banana came from and the soil web that sustained it. Next, offer gratitude to the hands that tended that tree and harvested it, and those people who helped get it to you. In a second example, if you are repairing your house, be grateful for the materials—where they came from, and what was given (the life of the tree for the board for your home). Also, express gratitude for the home that shelters you. Simply take the time to honor and acknowledge the earth that provided, the hands that provided, and be thankful. Or, if you harvested something directly, either from a garden you grew or from nature in the wild, be grateful. Before you harvest, ask permission. If you can, leave a small offering before you take anything. I like to use a pinch of homegrown herbs that I blend specifically for this purpose.

Try this practice as often as you can—I suggest committing to it for a week and seeing how it goes. Even if you don't do it for everything, start with one thing, like practicing deep gratitude at mealtimes or when you are getting yourself ready in the morning. If you do it some of the time, that is enough to help cultivate this gratitude within you. Consider also how you would express deep gratitude to the people in your life—those performing a service, those doing something nice, and take time to share.

Deep gratitude is a fundamentally transformational practice. It encourages you to slow down, pause, and be more aware of the relationship between you and the world around you. Being grateful makes things more meaningful, and our experience is richer for it. It roots us in the here and now and realigns our minds and hearts with the living earth.

Offerings as Gratitude

An additional way to express gratitude and respect is through the practice of offerings. Throughout time, humans have recognized that giving something back, physically or metaphysically, was important. Offerings are symbolic representations of gratitude and reciprocity we have with the earth that provides abundance. In some cultures, failure to make such offerings had dire consequences for those who depended on nature for survival: famine, pestilence, and so on might occur without proper offerings made. Other cultures had symbolic offerings to help bring a good harvest. Gratitude offerings can be done simply or with other aspects of ceremony (as we began to explore in chapter 1).

We can turn to the teachings of Indigenous North American tribes, including the six nations of the Haudenosaunee, for more on why gratitude matters. Chief Jake Swamp (Tekaronianeken) has delivered a Haudenosaunee Thanksgiving address or "words spoken before all others"[11] in many places, including at the United Nations, to help share why giving thanks is so important. As he shares, one of the reasons that gratitude is considered the first practice among the Indigenous North American tribes is that it is seen to literally rejuvenate and regenerate the land. In these traditional teachings, without gratitude, the land begins to wither and die. Thus, giving thanks is the very first thing that is done, before all others. Under this view, it is not just that humans as a whole have been taking too much from the living earth, but they have been doing it without the necessary gratitude that helps sustain and rejuvenate the land. Thus, gratitude practices are foundational to a healthy and functioning earth and why they can help heal our earth.

When would you make an offering? Offerings can be given anytime, and I suggest you build making into your core practices, something that you do when you interact with nature. But with that said, there are certainly times when it is a good idea to make offerings. It is good to make an offering anytime that you are asking for something from the living earth: if you are harvesting wild foods or vegetables from your garden; if you are asking for healing or energetic support from nature; or even if you are just visiting a new place. I like to make an offering to say "hello."

When it comes to offerings, I think that your intentions are what matter most—that you are genuine, that you have given the offering considerable thought, and that you offer something that is meaningful. Here are some options for what you can offer:

Offerings of Physical Things: You can offer something physical to the land, although you want to make sure whatever you are offering is meaningful, thoughtful, and not harmful. The general principle here that I like to follow is this: my offering should be something that holds value or represents a meaningful investment of time. Many things that can be purchased are problematic as offerings because they put additional strain on the land (the resources that produced it, the shipping and fossil fuels, the packaging, etc.). I believe it is better to either gather your offerings, make them, or grow them. They could be as simple as acorn caps that you have gathered in the fall, a sacred offering blend that you grew yourself and carry with you, a bit of mead that you brewed, a tomato you grew, or even a handful of birdseed.

Offerings as Rituals: Many offerings can also be ceremonial in nature; like a land blessing or healing ceremony. Ceremonies, such as many offered in this book can be wonderful gifts to the land. The gratitude mandala is one such example of an offering ritual (offered below).

Offerings of Creative Gifts: You can make an offering of gifts of your body and spirit: playing music, drumming, singing, chanting, or dancing. You can also create offerings of arts and crafts—grinding up stones to create paint, and painting symbols on stones, doing a wood-burned piece that is given to the trees, and so on. These can be gifts offered to the land itself, or gifts shown to humans in honor of and inspired by nature.

Offerings as Time and Life Energy: Anytime you are offering your time or life energy back to the land, that is a very powerful offering. We cover this more extensively in chapter 4: "Regeneration." Given the challenges we face, I believe that working to actively heal the land is one of the best offerings we can give.

As a specific example, I'll share some of my morning practices. I begin by getting up and getting ready to go outside to take care of our animals. As I brush my teeth, I think of the water coming out of the faucet and I am grateful for our spring. Then I step outside and take a moment just to breathe and be grateful I am alive. I greet the morning sun, thanking the sun for rising.

I look to my friends—the circle of plants, trees, wildlife, insects—and offer a blessing in the form of three "Awen" chants and say, "Thank you." I go about tending our bird flocks, greeting each person as they come out of their coops and wishing them a good day, offering treats. I perform my Sphere of Protection (a daily protective ritual practiced by the Ancient Order of Druids in America) and take a few moments to sit in the stillness of nature or take a ten minute walk on the paths around our land. I get myself dressed in my work clothes. I thank my car and ask for safety as I drive to work. As I drive, I radiate my love to the trees and mountains of my home, offering my gratitude. When I get there, I offer my gratitude to the big oak trees on my campus, and since if it rained overnight, check to the sidewalks and move any earthworms who may get stepped on. I put my hand on the old building, saying hello and entering the building. These small practices build on each other, but they share a basic foundational respect in acknowledging other beings, engaging with them as equals, and sharing my gratitude. They don't add much time to my day, but they certainly add a lot of connection and meaning.

RECIPROCATION

Gratitude and offerings are steps along the path of deepening our connection with the living earth, which ultimately puts us in a place of reciprocation. Reciprocation is about mutuality—respectful interaction where we both give and receive in thanks. Connections and relationships among all beings are built on trust and reciprocity. Reciprocity is the act of mutual exchange.

To learn reciprocity, we can first briefly talk about human culture, as this presents a good analogy for reciprocation with the land around you. Think about your close friends, family, and loved ones, and your relationships with them. Healthy, strong relationships are built on time spent together, shared connections, and doing nice things for each other—in other words, reciprocal interactions. Each party in the interaction gains something and also offers something. Relationships often break down when one party feels they are giving and not receiving. Currently, as we write this book, many Western cultures are experiencing a breakdown in civility and trust—and I would argue that one reason is because of the decline of reciprocity. You don't have to make peace with your neighbors if you can pay a specialist to come out and take care of whatever you need, rather than ask your neighbor for help. This creates an environment where we depend on money and other people's goods and services rather than our friends, neighbors, and ourselves. If there is no reciprocity, there is no actual reason for people to stay civil with each other. This is an important truth, and it speaks to the same kind of breakdown in the relationship between humans and the natural world.

Nature gives us humans everything she has to give. And at present, humans are taking more than she has to offer. She's holding up her end of the bargain of reciprocity as we are clothed, sheltered, kept warm, and fed. Humans have gotten into the habit of thinking that food and supplies come from shelves and stores, not nature. Large-scale systems of extraction, harvest, and distribution mask the reality that has never changed: literally, everything we have comes from the living earth. Because of these broader systems at play, reciprocation is something that has to be taught and carefully learned—and it takes intentional actions. Thus, we humans have forgotten that this is a *relationship*—and practicing reciprocity helps us get back into this connection. If we never learn how to interact and use nature—ethically, thoughtfully, and with gratitude—we are never going to develop deep and abiding connections with her.

How do we practice reciprocation? Recognizing first and foremost that you are in a relationship with nature, and that that relationship needs to be tended. Tend your relationship with nature by doing things for nature and recognize that you can give back as much as you are taking. Balance what you take with what you give, and make sure you are always in a place of gratitude and seeking permission for what is both given and taken.

One other thing is important to note here: reciprocation is not a scorecard. If nature is always giving to us, we can work back to give to nature as much as we can. We can live our lives in ways that honor nature, revere her, and offer reciprocation through the life choices we make as well as how we directly help support the living earth. This can look very different for those in different walks of life. Here are several to consider:

- **Lifestyle choices:** Because so many human-driven systems at present are destructive of life, lifestyle choices are an excellent place to begin a larger practice of reciprocation. Thus, finding ways to minimize your impact on the living earth and even work to heal her through your choices can be impactful and meaningful. This can be anything from shifting your choices of transportation or eliminating one-use plastics to growing your own food or learning composting.[12]

- **Engaging in the work of regeneration.** Because our lands have been so damaged both historically by colonial systems and at present by large-scale resource extraction, anything that you can do to directly support the health of local ecosystems and species is incredible and respectful. Chapter 4: "Regeneration," describes this work in detail.

- **Providing support to others doing this work.** Providing your time, voice, or funds to support good organizations that are doing regenerative, earth-protecting, or rewilding work can be another excellent option.
- **Teaching others about these practices.** If we are to sustain a more positive vision for the future, part of this work involves bringing many more humans back into healthy, sustaining relationships with nature. Thus, another approach is teaching people to build their own relationships with the land around them—especially younger generations.
- **Identifying the differences between needs and wants and embracing simple living.** If we are able to ask less from the earth, this is another form of reciprocation and respect. Identifying what is a need for us versus what is a want, repairing and reusing, and working to eliminate the purchasing of new unnecessary goods can be another very powerful method of reciprocation. We put less strain and demands on the earth when we consume less.

A simple example here can help illustrate some of these changes. On our homestead, we have an herb garden that we converted from lawn—we used all local materials and "waste" materials (fall leaves, our own compost, wood, and local stone) to build up our herb beds. This is a place where we engage in regular ceremonies for the earth. When I come home from work, I go to the herb garden. I want to make some smoke-cleansing sticks for my practice with Mugwort, Sage, Rosemary, and Lavender. I greet the garden as I enter, basket and tools in hand. I sit next to Sage and say, "Dear wise one, you look beautiful today and are growing so tall. Is there anything I can do for you?" Sage suggests that she might benefit from some compost and mulch, so I bring over more compost and mulch and do a little light weeding (the weeds and I have an agreement about where they can grow, and that is not in the garden bed). After tending her, I say, "Sage, I am in need of your healing. May I cut back some of you for my smoke-clearing sticks?" She agrees, and I ask, "How much?" I use my inner listening skills to determine how much she is willing to have me take, and I cut back the plant carefully. I offer my gratitude by singing to her and later, by painting a beautiful rendition of a sage plant, which I share with others with a story. I make my smoke-clearing sticks for my personal use and to share with friends.

As we come to our conclusion of the triad of these practices, there is one more thing to mention. Part of why respect-based practices get left out of our conversations and discussions is also due to the nature of present-day, fast-paced culture. We are often so busy moving from thing to thing that we do not take the necessary time to step back and be respectful. But I hope, as this chapter is shared, regardless of how busy you are, you can make time for these core practices. They do not take long and bring us into alignment with nature and spirit.

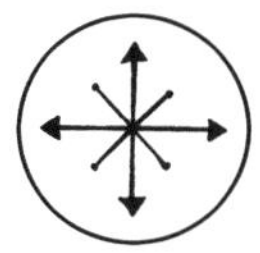

Story of the Present:

REJECTING COLONIALISM

After 500 years of colonialism, the peoples of earth have had enough. People begin to engage in re-indigenization and decolonizing work on every level, challenging the systems of power and extraction that have for too long shaped and guided planetary history. This is hard, brutal, and often painful work, and is often met with resistance by those larger systems of power. And yet, day by day, more and more individuals join this larger movement from all walks of life. People begin to embrace local knowledge and local ways of thinking and doing, recognizing the value in their unique circumstances and perspectives. A special emphasis on local foods, foodways, and growing one's own food begins to move into the mainstream. Even the smallest of rural communities now has a bustling farmer's market, which shares not only locally produced goods but also local crafts, music, and culture.

As nature is presently in peril, more and more people work to fight, preserve, and protect nature, both by changing their own lifestyles and by joining together to protect and replant broader lands. A network of refugia is being created all over the world to create sanctuaries for life. A rekindled emphasis on nature spirituality and honoring nature also becomes central, and even global monotheistic religions see value in honoring and respecting the earth. Indigenous voices and others who have been systematically oppressed and silenced are given honored places in communities and in broader cultures where they are able to share their knowledge and offer a different path forward. Indigenous peoples are also to reclaim their lands and openly practice previously oppressed traditions, lifeways, and languages. A movement that seems so small at first grows and grows until it is bursting at the seams, and the peoples of Earth realize that this is a better, more respectful way forward.

Respect as a Bard

INTERACTIONS, FOOD, AND HOSTING

Respectful practices don't just have power in the natural world, they also have power in our human communities, cultures, and creative practices. Building respectful interactions can impact every aspect of our lives and benefit all around us. Thus, we now explore some of the ways we can bring these kinds of practices into our human communities.

Respectful Interactions in our Human Communities

Just as we work on the triad of gratitude in our interactions with nature, so, too, can our communities and our own relationships benefit greatly from this work. At the time of writing this book, our human communities on a global scale are deeply fragmented; many countries are now seeing more political polarization than at any time in recent history, with opposing parties refusing to speak or interact with those of a different perspective. Communication has broken down on a fundamental level. We are also seeing an increase in violent uprisings, shootings, and human-against-human violence, speaking a need for a different path. Respect-based practices, including gratitude and reciprocation, can help rebuild relationships and trust in our human communities.

Adopting a gratitude practice in your interactions with other people can help foster positive interactions with others and, in time, build stronger and more connected human communities. As a first step, consider working to offer gratitude to people you interact with in your day-to-day life. For example, people in service industries are often paid for their work, but a little bit of gratitude goes a long way. Take the time in your workplace to thank people for their hard work, their contributions, and the work they do. Take time to regularly thank your loved ones for their role in your life. This very simple practice can brighten someone's day and bring connection and joy. Consider also how you can model these practices for others—teaching respectful interaction to younger generations, in particular, can be a very valuable approach.

Gratitude in Food and Foodways

A powerful place where communities and nature intersect is through food and mealtimes. This can be a place to begin a set of powerful respect-oriented practices in our human communities—right around our own dinner tables.

Just as we explored breaking bread with each other in chapter 1, we can deepen that practice here with the following:

- **Beginning a meal in gratitude.** Begin each meal in gratitude, taking a moment for each person at the table to share something that they are grateful for in their day. Then, take a moment to share gratitude for the earth and the hands that prepared the meal. This can be anything that you choose it to be, including something as simple as "Thank you to the earth for the food I am about to eat."
- **Deep gratitude in cooking.** As you prepare a meal, take time to slow down and thank each ingredient when you cook. Also pause and thank your tools, the appliances or the fire you are using for cooking, and anything else you interact with. See how this practice of deep gratitude changes your cooking experience and how it changes the energy of the meal.
- **Offerings and spirit plates.** Another common tradition in neopaganism, drawn from older traditions, is the spirit plate. A spirit plate is a small plate that is made for the spirits—household spirits, land spirits, ancestor spirits, deities, or whoever else you may want to honor. A small bite of each part of the meal is offered, and then the plate can be placed on an altar or left outside. The spirits metaphysically consume the energy of the food, and then, you can leave it for wildlife and/or compost the physical remnants.

If you grow any of your own food or participate in a community garden or urban garden, you can build a rich set of respect-oriented practices into your yearly cycle of planting, sowing, and harvesting. Consider a permanent altar in your garden—a place to make offerings and dedicate to the spirits of the land, the spirits of the vegetable, herb, nut, and fruit plants that are sustaining you. You can offer ceremonies at the beginning and end of the growing seasons, again focusing on gratitude.

Good Host and Good Guest Traditions

Another approach to building more respectful interactions can be found in the many ancient global traditions for both being a good host and a good guest. Some of these traditions, also surround certain times of the year, such as offering gifts and honoring the first guest in the home each year. For example, in Slavic lore, the "first foot" traditions often include a young man (representing a radiant spring God such as Radagast) who comes as the first guest through the door after the winter solstice bringing a gift of grain.[13] This young guest's magical offering brings a blessing to the home through the full year. Throughout the world, many traditions continue to persist surround respectful interactions when someone is entering, staying, or hosting guests although in modern time these traditions are being lost.

As one way of building respectful interactions with others, you might consider both your role as a good host and a good guest, drawing upon the traditions of your own culture or building new traditions as you see fit. As a host, consider the ways in which you create a comfortable space, greet and welcome your guests, make them feel at home, tend to their needs, offer them food and drink, and engage in conversation. As a guest, consider the gifts you might bring, how you might conduct yourself when staying at their home, how you can help the host with your visit, and so forth. Many of these older traditions have been lost in the modern age, and with them, the magic that they wove between human beings and communities.

Respect as a Druid

ANIMISM, PERMISSION, AND SOVEREIGNTY

Now that we've explored respectful practices with nature and human communities, we turn to the more esoteric and magical aspects of respect. To begin that discussion, let's start by unpacking some more terms that we will explore in this chapter. As we examined above, *Respect* involves both admiration and noninterference or the acknowledgment of a being's sovereignty. In other words, respect is not just about liking something or feeling good about it, but through that admiration, recognizing that a thing has a right to life and to exist on its own terms. *Gratitude* is one way of acting on that respect through being thankful, offering appreciation, making offerings, or showing other kindness. *Honoring* or *reverence* takes these basics a step further; when we honor or revere someone or something, we demonstrate great respect and admiration. Finally, *reciprocation* is about equal and mutual exchange, where each party is providing to the others and there is mutuality in relationship. In order to create building blocks toward respect of nature and frame the rest of this chapter, we now delve into animistic philosophy.

Cosmology: Animism

As we began to see with my description of my interaction with the Sage plant above, I spoke with the spirit of the plant in order to gain permission to harvest and use the plant for my needs. This is a simple example of animism. Animism is a belief in the spirit of all things. Animistic views recognize that rivers, stones, trees, animals, even human-created objects, and people all have spirits and that those spirits can be worked with, learned from, and honored in various ways. That is, animism applies to everything in the world—since all things come from nature. And as we will explore in this section, an animistic philosophy helps us understand the true power and meaning of respect, including the respect for the sovereignty of all beings. Historical evidence suggests that before the rise of modern human civilizations, it is likely that most peoples of the world held animistic philosophies. That is, nearly all cultures' Indigenous beliefs are animistic in nature,[14] even if they may also recognize deities and other larger spirits. Animism continues to be foundational to current Indigenous people's beliefs globally and is a growing important movement in modern-day nature spirituality. When colonization took place in many parts of the world, Indigenous traditions, nearly all of which have their basis in animism, were suppressed and eradicated. So, in exploring animism, we are drawing upon this ancient wisdom in all of our ancient human roots to be able to help humans return to a more balanced interaction with nature.

Animism is the foundational spiritual practice of religious belief. It is intimately connected to cultures that have a healthy, thriving relationship with the biosphere and it is in opposition to the never-ending, consumeristic consumption characterized by cultures that adhere to a model that is solely scientific, materialistic, and reductionist. After all, it's much harder to cut down a tree or destroy a whole forest if they are your friends.

Further, there seems to be compelling evidence that animism is the original human spiritual tradition. It is found worldwide, both historically and in contemporary deeply nature-connected cultures. Some had tried to portray this as a "primitive" stage of religious development that reinforces social evolutionary models and hierarchies based in racist and colonial beliefs. Instead, perhaps it is time to acknowledge that even in the major world religions, both monotheistic and polytheistic, you find elements of animism in subcultures of those traditions that live in close harmony with nature. Examples include Tibetan Buddhism; the jungle traditions of Buddhism of Southeast Asia; the nature spirituality of Celtic Christian monks; the syncretic traditions of Christian and Indigenous belief in Central and South America; the intermingling of Hindu, Islamic, and Animist beliefs in Bali; and some aspects of Sufi practice. While animism may take different forms in different cultures, animism (which is part of current nature-based spiritual movements) has some common threads. Lots of different interpretations exist, so this list might look a little different for different groups or animists, but here are some common beliefs:

- Recognizing and honoring the spirits in things present in the world and universe, both animate and inanimate, both natural and created
- Recognizing the importance of interacting respectfully with those spirits; building the right relationships and connections with them and learning from them as teachers and guides
- Recognizing that our actions have a significant impact on all other beings and that we can engage in right actions to behave in ways that honor the sovereignty of all beings
- Recognizing that humans are part of nature, like any other animal, and that we have a set of tools we have evolved to interact with other beings, including our five senses as well as instinct and intuition
- Recognizing that we have to cultivate our own intuition, observation, and listening skills (inner and outer) so that we might effectively communicate with the spirit present in all things
- Recognizing that humans' primary role on this planet is that of caretakers or custodians, here to tend the land, not exploit it

Let's take some time to walk through the above list. The very first item on the list is the basic assumption of animism: the world is full of spirits. Not only do living beings like humans, fish, and insects have spirits, but all natural beings in the world, like mountains, rivers, and oceans also have spirits. This begins the separation from a colonial mindset—by recognizing the inherent spirit in all things, it fundamentally changes our interaction with the land around us. If we see nature not as a resource to extract and do with what we please, but rather, we see the entirety of nature as an enchanted world of spirit full of nonhuman persons with their own sovereignty, then every interaction requires respect.

Since everything in the world has a spirit and humans also have a spirit, this moves into the spirit of human-created objects. Thus, when spirit-filled humans transform raw, spirit-filled materials into objects like phones, cars, or houses, those also have spirit. This means that on a daily basis, every person, place, or thing we interact with has a spirit. Some people can get caught up in whether or not human-created things have spirits, but as soon as they open their hearts to listen, they will hear the voices of these spirits too. And this also matters—in a world where everything is designed to be quickly consumed and thrown away, if we accept that things like disposable plastic or our cell phones also have spirits, this too changes our interaction.

Moving on to our second point, a belief in animism recognizes that we can interact with the world of spirits in meaningful and respectful ways. In fact, a great deal of earth-based, Indigenous, and nature-centered spiritual practices across cultures focus on creating safe, effective, and reverent ways of engaging in this interaction. Meditations, ceremonies, spiritual practices, offerings, and many other practices were—and for those who are animists, today are—rooted in establishing and maintaining right relationships with spirits. For example, the modern-day Wassailing ceremony, which is an apple orchard blessing that came out of Europe, is animistic in nature. People gather around the tree, make offerings, sing songs to support the apple orchard, and make noise to drive bad spirits from the tree. Respect, gratitude, and reverence are cornerstones of how to engage in respectful interaction and therefore gain a good harvest, which allows people to thrive in the cold winter months.

This brings us to our third item on the list—we human beings have had a significant impact on the world of matter, and therefore, the world of spirit. Unfortunately, due to colonialism and its prevailing attitudes in the last five centuries, humans have had many negative impacts on the world, leading to the present crisis. Part of the work we have to do to build a brighter future is to realign our relationship with that world of spirits, particularly those of the living earth, and learn how to engage in more respectful interaction. This gets into much of the work of this book—the 7 R's must be built on a foundation of respect.

Our final three principles on the list are about recognizing our own role and human birthright. We humans are spirit-filled ourselves, we are part of nature, and many, many millennia ago, we have evolved the necessary senses and tools—including our instincts and intuition (explored more in chapter 6)—to give us everything that we need to interact in the world of spirits. However, most of us grew up in cultures that often refuse to acknowledge the spirit of things, and because of that, we often have self-imposed or cultural blocks on our natural abilities that we need to fully interact with the world of spirits.

Further, as Tyson Yunkaporta shares in *Sand Talk: How Indigenous Thinking Can Save the World*,[15] humans have a very specific role in the world: custodians or caretakers of the living earth. Due to humanity's gifts and skills, we are meant to tend, care for, and nurture life on earth—and when we are in this role, we are at our best. Of course, this is the opposite role that many humans have created for themselves in the present era or previous eras. For too long, humans of the west have seen nature not as something to protect, preserve, and defend but rather as something to extract, colonize, and destroy. I am not surprised that in this current role as extractors of nature, we are full of sickness, disease, mental illness, and general malaise—because we have lost our core work and true purpose on earth. This is why it feels so good to get in the garden, to go plant trees, to spend time in nature, or to do any other earth-honoring activity. When we do these things, we return to our original purpose, and our human spirit resonates deeply with this original role. Thus, part of respect for nature asks us to claim and enact the role of being a custodian, caretaker, and guardian of the living earth. To be in a relationship with nature in a powerful way and allow that mutuality to drive our decisions and thought processes.

What is beautiful about the framing of humans as caretakers is that it gives us a new, powerful way to be a human in a way that matters deeply right now. It gives us purpose and restructures our relationship with nature as one filled with care. Many of the present cultural narratives surrounding humans and their impact on the world are almost entirely negative. Ben Falk, in the film *Inhabit*,[16] shares this perspective at the beginning of the film. He argues that the green and environmental movements usually focus on lessening human impacts on the living earth, sharing how human impact is always a bad thing. By this line of reasoning, the best thing you can do is not exist because the earth would be better without you and your impact. But, what if instead we had tools like rewilding (see chapter 3) and regeneration (explored in chapter 4) to create positive impacts? Being caretakers, tenders, and honoring the land—through the deep interaction with spirits, through the 7 R's covered in this book—can help us make that shift. We can be a force of good and a force of healing.

We can reclaim our original birthright as human beings and bring forth a better vision for tomorrow. And we can move away from colonial mindsets into a place of what Robin Wall Kimmerer in *Braiding Sweetgrass*[17] calls becoming "naturalized to place" and returning to the beliefs, systems, and nature-centered lifeways of our ancient ancestors. Stepping back, this is an ambitious list to begin to consider, much less adopt. Moving into an animist practice takes a lot of time, dedication, thinking, and action to take us from the colonial mindset into a place of respect, and ultimately care, for nature. To embrace animism, we not only have to attend to both our inner and outer selves, but to both our foundational beliefs and assumptions about the world and how those beliefs and assumptions are practiced through our actions. This work is very difficult, both because it takes time for that kind of reorientation, and because we are moving in the opposite direction of many present cultural norms and practices. But, being willing to walk down the path, and having enough of us decide to go in that direction means we can change the present and the future.

Permission and Sovereignty

As we have begun to explore in our activities above, learning respectful interaction requires that you treat the world of nature—all spirits—as the sovereign, equal beings that they are. The easiest way of thinking about and engaging with respectful interaction with all spirits is by recognizing that other being (whether is is a tree, a stone, your lawn you want to convert into a garden) as a sovereign being with their own opinions, needs, desires, and lives. In the same way that you would not walk up to a human stranger and give them a hug, cut their hair, or take their purse without permission, you can apply this same knowledge to the world of spirits. Thus, before you do anything, ask for permission. For example, before you forage for wild berries, take a moment to ask if you can harvest from the berry bush. As you harvest, recognize that this is a sovereign being, and do everything you can to honor that being, taking only what the berry bush is willing to offer. If you have to cut a tree down because they are in danger of falling on your house, speak with that tree, make offerings, and seek permission. Listen to what the spirits of nature tell you in response—and heed what they say.

If a being says "no" to you, respect that response. Leave, come back later, and ask again at another time, or recognize that maybe the being is simply not interested and move on. Respect the sovereignty of that being and the right for them to make their own choices. Not regarding the spirits' desires is disrespectful, and it will mark you as a human who they may not want to deal with. Too many humans do not listen to the voices or nature, and take what they want, and through their actions, cause nature to come to harm. Thus, the "no" may be a test to see what kind of human you are—one who listens? One who takes? One who honors? This is foundational and will impact your entire relationship with the living earth.

While what I've written here seems straightforward, I can tell you from almost twenty years of animist practices, it is easier said than done. Those—like me—who have grown up in Western cultures may have a lifetime of cultural conditioning to undo and overcome. This conditioning insists that humans are superior and that we can take what we want from land we own or from the living earth—sometimes this conditioning is subconscious, and we end up having to take a long time to undo it. This means we may make mistakes and that can lead to us taking and doing things without permission. We may get excited or forget to ask. The good news is that once you start these practices, the spirits understand that you are learning, you are growing, and that you make mistakes. Mistakes for me most often come when I'm out foraging and I get super excited when find a giant mushroom patch and jump in to harvest without taking a moment for permission and gratitude—then I have to say, "I'm sorry," back up, take a moment, and remember my core practices of respect. Work at it, and it will come.

Meditation and Opening Your Heart to the Spirits of Nature

In order to open ourselves up to the voices of spirits and of nature and begin walking an animist path, we often need to do some foundational work. Due to the cultural conditioning many of us experience, our minds and hearts are very closed. Screens fill our brains daily with nonsense that disconnects us, there is often not room for anything else. Just like planting seeds, we want the soil we are cultivating to be rich and fertile so that our interactions with the world of spirit can bear fruit—and this preparatory work can help with that.

Basic Mind-Clearing Meditation. One of the most fundamental practices for learning how to listen to the voices of the spirits is to practice some form of regular meditation. Even five minutes a day will show substantial results. The meditation offered is a basic mind-clearing meditation, allowing you to quiet your mind. You can do this practice outdoors or indoors. For indoors, you can use a lit candle. If you are going outdoors, select somewhere natural to sit and be present in nature—your Sit Spot, as described in chapter 1, is an excellent choice.

Begin by focusing on your breath. Breathe in for a count of four, hold lightly for a count of four, breathe out for a count of four, and hold lightly (this is taught as box breath or fourfold breath). Continue to do this three or more times, and then when you feel ready, quiet your breath, letting it return to normal. Simply focus on the candle or nature around you and continue to breathe. If thoughts come to the surface, acknowledge them and then allow them to settle out of your awareness. What this basic practice does is it allows you to learn to quiet your mind and create space for silence. Within that silence, the voices of spirits—rather than the voices of our culture—have space to share. This also allows you to increase your focus, which is a critical skill for any spirit work. One of the reasons this kind of meditation works is that if our heads are so full of our own thoughts, it can become very difficult for the spirits of all other beings to share. We have to quiet our own minds, turn off the screens and voices of human culture, and open ourselves to the quiet wisdom of the spirits of nature.

Voices of Nature Exercises. The spirits of the world—present in all things—are ready and excited to communicate with us. They haven't forgotten who we are meant to be as a species, and they are ready to guide us on this path again. We just have to be ready to listen. The first time you do this exercise, I suggest doing it with a tree or plant that has a lot of human interaction and tending (a medicinal herb like Sage or Rosemary, a tree that produces nuts or fruit, or vegetables in your garden). That's because certain plant species have long-term relationships with humans and are more attuned to our energies, making this initial interaction easier. Eventually, you can broaden to talk to many other living things.

Begin by asking permission to sit next to the plant or tree. Ask for permission internally or aloud and wait for a response. Communication from nature is not necessarily verbal. Messages may come in both inner and outer ways and may be tied to any one of your senses: leaves blowing in the wind, an intuitive sense, a good fuzzy feeling in your gut, hearing a "yes" response, and so on. Once you have an affirmative sign, sit down near the plant or tree and offer gratitude (see below for more on permission and gratitude). Nature and spirit interactions should always begin with permission and gratitude. If the being says no, honor the sovereignty of that being, offer your gratitude, and find a different plant or return a different day and ask again. Often a "no" is a test—to see if you respect the spirits of nature and are willing to honor them.

Assuming you have permission to move forward at this time, take a moment to quiet your mind. Then, when you are ready, say hello. Wait for a response, and then continue to communicate. It may take you some time to get a response, but you will get a response. Interact. Build a relationship with this being. Learn how this being communicates. Hear their heartbeat and the song of their leaves on the wind. Use all of your senses to learn from this being. Learn from them through mutual exchange, recognizing the sovereignty of this being and the teachings they may have to offer. I suggest working with this being and building this relationship for some time. When you are ready, start talking to other beings. Eventually, with practice, you will be able to communicate with natural beings as easily as you can communicate with human beings.

Expanding Your Sphere Outward. Once you've begun to talk to a few of the local plant and animal spirits, you are well on your way to building relationships with the spirits of the land. Allow this to unfold in a natural way, meeting new spirits, talking with them, making offerings (see the rest of this chapter), and building relationships. Like any set of relationships, it takes time and meaningful interactions. Recognize that adapting an animist philosophy is a process, and part of your work is not just learning how to interact respectfully, but also how to address unconscious and semiconscious behaviors present in these interactions. Often people find it easiest at first to communicate and connect with the different elements of nature such as trees, plants, rocks, rivers, the sky, or the wind. Then perhaps, you can broaden your experience by reaching out to engage in respectful interaction with things like our houses, cars, tools, and even computers and smartphones.

Getting to Know the Local Spirits. From there, the sky is the limit. Start interacting with the beings of the natural world or human-created world in whatever ways you feel led. Greet and engage in "conversation" with the trees, animals, plants, and other beings where you live. This can be out loud or internally as well. Learn to listen deeply. Pay attention to your dreams and note which, if any, members of your bioregion show up in your dreams.

Always remember to work with all beings with gratitude and respect. Let them be your teachers, your guides, and learn from them. They have so much wisdom to share, and they can teach us everything we need to know. Every bit of time that you invest in a practice like this is time well spent.

I will end this entire chapter by saying that the work outlined here is difficult because it requires unlearning not only automatic behaviors but also examining fundamental assumptions that most of us grow up with and ideologies that we have never examined before. It is also critical work for all of us to bring forth a new paradigm, the work of this lifetime—learning, growing, and beginning to recognize our place in this interconnected world full of spirits. While it takes time, and you will likely make many mistakes, it is critical to bringing forth a better future for all life.

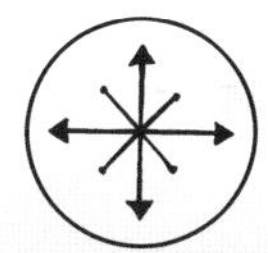

Story of the Future:

FREEDOM RESTORED

A group of people stands in ceremony on a tall mountain, overlooking a lush, abundant forested valley in Eastern North America. The land is once again a rich and verdant food forest. Small communities live in harmony with nature, and the land is so abundant that it can easily feed all who live within—human or otherwise—with its rich forests full of chestnuts, acorns, berries, hazelnuts, apples, roots and tubers, and game. Gone but never forgotten are the practices of colonialization and oppression. In fact, these attitudes are often described in the people's stories of the times before, recognizing that cultures and communities must protect against the darker nature of humans as it manifests through greed, dominion, and narcissism. As these future humans stand once again on a verdant and abundant landscape, they celebrate this day as a day of gratitude toward their human ancestors. They recognize the work of their ancestors walking the difficult path back toward ecological balance and respectful interactions with nature. Due to the hard work of these and many other ancestors, and with the support of the spirits of the land, humanity has once again returned to health, balance, and joy.

Freedom Joy Growth Liberation
BARD
gathering around the fire, creative practices, wild movement
OVATE
Natural Rhythms, Rewilding ecosystems & communities, rewilding our lives
DRUID
genus Loci
WILD OFFERINGS
WILD MEDITATION & CEREMONY
REWILDING

CHAPTER 3

Rewilding

With Nate Summers

Story of the Past:

ABUNDANCE LOST

The world was once full of life on a scale we can't even imagine. On Turtle Island (North America), just a few centuries ago, bison roamed the Great Plains in massive herds numbering in the millions. People nomadically followed these herds, hunting and living off a deep, wild, intimate relationship with the giant animals.

Wolves and grizzly bears lived all across the continent, coexisting with human populations for millennia. In the Northeast, the passenger pigeons were so numerous that when they migrated, their numbers would block out the sun. The population was so great that it was said you could throw a stone into the sky and hit one bird on the way up and another one on the way down. This is the origin of the saying "Two birds with one stone." Along the West Coast of the continent, seasonal migrations of salmon were so extensive that when the salmon runs were happening on the rivers, it looked as if you could walk across the backs of the salmon to reach the other side. Often, tribal people who lived off the salmon could harvest enough food for the wintertime in a matter of days. Similarly large numbers of wild and large animals roamed other continents as well, including the aurochs, wolves, bison, and leopards of Europe.

Things changed.

Bison were deliberately slaughtered to the borderline of extinction, limited to a vastly reduced range of their former population. Passenger pigeons were hunted out of existence. Salmon populations were decimated through overfishing, habitat loss, and the creation of dams. Wolves were extirpated both from Europe and most of the southern part of Turtle Island. The leopards and bison of Europe both went extinct, and aurochs almost disappeared.

INTRODUCING REWILDING

The reintroduction of wolves to the Greater Yellowstone Ecosystem had a much-bigger impact than anyone had anticipated. Wolves had been hunted to extinction in the Lower 48 states (except for select areas of Minnesota), and in January 1995 they were deliberately reintroduced. A few decades later, not only were there healthy wolf populations all over Yellowstone National Park and the surrounding area, but entire ecosystems that had been devastated were restored.

As humans, it's difficult for us to truly understand the effects that happen when we remove a major predator from a healthy intact ecosystem, let alone when we remove dozens or hundreds. Yet, people have started paying attention and are reintroducing major species that have been extirpated (effectively extinct in areas of their natural habitat). This is not just the case for animals either.

Rewilding has started to take the world by storm in a variety of ways, both in nature and human culture. But what does it mean to rewild a specific species? And are humans in need of rewilding? In this sense, Rewilding may mean the reintroduction of certain species, allowing fallow areas to reforest, or deliberately returning a certain area back into its natural state through replanting and restoration. In the United States, Rewilding is often used as a term related more directly to humans and our own behavior. This version of Rewilding suggests that we human beings have become overly domesticated and are suffering in a zoo-like cage we have built for ourselves called civilization.[18]

How can we reconcile these different meanings? Well, one way to define Rewilding is to consider it ***the returning of a place, ecosystem, animal, or even human to its natural wild state***. Implicit here is the idea of undoing domestication or at least overdomestication. Embedded within an understanding of Rewilding are ideas of **freedom, wildness, naturalness, and vitality**. This is the state to which things return or develop when not overburdened with the forces of domestication.

As human beings, if we spent over 200,000 years wandering the earth as hunter-gatherers with nomadic tendencies, in a land filled with abundant nature all around us, might it not be a little strange for us to spend most of our time now inside, looking at screens, and in urban areas almost devoid of nature? What if the widespread mental health issues we now face, such as anxiety, depression, and large amounts of stress, have something to do with our brains expecting more plants, trees, birds, mammals, fish, reptiles, amphibians, and so forth in our lives? What if today the major diseases we face, such as obesity, diabetes, heart disease, and cancer, are actually connected to an overly sedentary lifestyle brought about by human domestication?

Can we as humans Rewild ourselves? And, if we are to truly ReVision the future, then we need to Rewild the world as part of that as well. In this chapter, we will look at both of these approaches: Rewilding nature, the biosphere, and ecosystems, and simultaneously seeking to Rewild our human lives and cultures. Rewilding allows us to understand that we are part of nature, that we belong to nature and can be part of wild places. We can create wild places within our own homes and communities, and we can realign ourselves with the wilderness within and without.

Rewilding as an Ovate

ECOSYSTEMS, COMMUNITIES, AND NATURAL CYCLES

Looking through the lens of the Ovate and our focus on nature and nature studies, we find that Rewilding is a ripe concept to apply to our lives to help *ReVision* the world and the future. Here, the idea of a fractal, a geometric pattern that replicates both at micro- and macroscopic scale, is helpful as a tool to look at the scope and range of what we might accomplish. We can Rewild on a broad scale at the global and bioregional level, while simultaneously Rewilding our backyards, our gardens, and our relationship with the foods we eat. This is both an ecological, scientific principle found in nature (like how sap moving through a tree, blood moving through the body, and water moving through the land all resemble each other) and also an example of the magical idea of "As above, so below, as within, so without." Here are some examples of what Rewilding can look like:

- Removing dams and levees and allowing water systems to follow their natural flow, as well as allowing natural aquatic habitats to reestablish

- Restoring native plants and habitat to large areas such as the prairie of North America. This simultaneously benefits animals by giving them back their natural habitat and also reduces the uses of chemical herbicides and pesticides, thus benefiting pollinator species. At the same time, global climate change can be mitigated through carbon sequestration, since the reintroduced native plants will sink more carbon into the soil.

- Stopping fishing in certain zones in the ocean, lakes, or rivers to allow fish populations and other marine organisms to rebound

- Reintroducing apex predators and keystone species to their natural habitats to help restore ecological balance in an area (e.g., wolves in Yellowstone)

- Establishing new areas and letting old areas go completely wild and return to their natural ecological state

Rewilding Ecosystems

When facing the task of Rewilding entire ecosystems and the biosphere, the enormity of the task can be a little overwhelming. A full two-thirds of the entire wild earth has now been lost to development and agriculture, and most of that has happened in just the last seventy years (this includes oceans)! Only one-third of the planet is still left as natural habitat and wild, free space for animals and plants to grow and thrive as they are naturally meant to.

Fortunately, we are at a moment in history when the *beginning* of Rewilding ecosystems is happening in *some* places. In Europe, for the first time in what is likely hundreds of years, several different areas are being allowed to reforest naturally on their own, and wildlife is returning. This has also happened *accidentally* in places such as Chernobyl, where radioactivity has prevented human occupation.[19]

There are also projects happening all over the world around reintroducing animal or plant species that are either severely threatened or have disappeared altogether from their traditional range. Probably the easiest way for us to participate and support this form of Rewilding (besides contributing financially to organizations who do this work) is to get involved with ***Ecological Restoration*** work in our local area. Contributing to this kind of work doesn't mean you have to change careers. Volunteer helpers make a huge impact on ecological restoration work around the world. This can involve everything from tree planting and native plant restoration to wildlife monitoring, invasive-species removal, and even simply cleaning up trash at a local park.

While this way of contributing might seem to be a "drop in the bucket," it is actually hugely significant, and it is one of the main ways that we can make a very specific impact on the health of the biosphere for the future. Check with local conservation groups, tribal groups, and environmental organizations to find out how a little bit of your dirt time and sweat can help rewild the land around you. In chapter 4, "Regeneration," we offer many approaches to participate in ecological restoration.

Rewilding Our Cities, Towns, and Neighborhoods

The importance of wilderness for the health of our planet cannot be overstated. There is a desperate need for wild places around the world, with minimal or even no human use and intervention. This allows wildlife and ecosystems to thrive, repopulate, and find their own natural rhythms and patterns. Increasing the number and size of wilderness areas is a worthy goal. But what about the rest of the world? What about the areas that humans already occupy? Can we Rewild those spaces as well?

The simple answer is yes. While the rate of development, deforestation, and home building continues at unprecedented rates all over the world, there are also approaches happening where people are consciously incorporating rewilding ideas into cities, towns, and neighborhoods. For instance, in Singapore over the last decade, the government has rewilded and regreened its city-state by consciously incorporating native vegetation into its urban and building design. Trees and plants are grown all over rooftops and buildings, and green corridors travel throughout the city. This has resulted in an overall cooling effect on the city, driving down energy costs, and it has also resulted in the reemergence and repopulation of wildlife into the city.

In other places, wildlife corridors are increasingly being built to connect different habitats for wildlife. This includes green spaces in cities, wildlife over- and underpasses around interstate highways, and the linking together of park systems on a regional scale never before imagined. The hoped-for result is a rebounding of wildlife and native plant populations.

It seems as if there is a real possibility of incorporating ecological, wildlife, and rewilding principles into urban design in order to benefit humans, wildlife, and the planet. We all can contribute by supporting organizations involved in this work, working at the local level, and even participating in this Rewild design approach through public input on existing and future projects. Here are some specific ways to help in and around where you live:

- Organize and help with tree planting.
- Participate or start native plant restoration projects.
- Work toward protecting and increasing green spaces, including trails, parks, and green projects (such as green rooftops in cities).
- Create, design, and implement a community food forest.
- Help create a community medicinal-plant or native-plant garden.
- Participate and support wildlife-monitoring projects and wildlife corridor and habitat creation.
- Focus on removing lawns and bringing back native vegetation.

Rewilding Our Yards

It should come as no surprise that our homes and yards are some of the areas of highest domestication; after all, they're *domestic*. But as we face the ecological crises of the twenty-first century, perhaps it is time to look a little deeper at our most-intimate spaces and if perhaps they might be Rewilded as well.

In our fourth chapter, "Regeneration," we will look at the concept of a yarden—the idea of transforming our yards into gardens. This idea may appeal to most of us, or not, but it is clear that our lawns are one of the biggest sources of ecological challenge most immediate to us. They are hotbeds of toxic chemicals in the forms of petroleum-derived herbicides, pesticides, and fertilizers. Mowing our yards weekly uses a ton of energy in terms of fossil fuels, while suppressing the growth of mature vegetation, especially including native plants. In fact, if you think about it for a moment, keeping a lawn is actually forcing the area around your home *not* to be in whatever its natural ecological state might be.

So, can we rewild our lawns and yards? The simple answer is yes, and it might be one of the most powerful actions we can take. Believe it or not, our yards are actually crucial habitat for pollinators, other insects, and birds. The dramatic drops in bird and insect populations are directly tied to loss of habitat from areas being converted to the ecological death zones we call lawns. In my neighborhood, it's not uncommon for pesticide companies to come calling once or twice a year, promising an "eco-friendly" way to get rid of all the bees, spiders, and other pesky invertebrates. They are usually quite shocked when we let them know we are actually quite happy with the pollinators that come to our yard every year, and we actually are happy with the spiders too!

By simply allowing sections (sections, not the whole yard) of my simple suburban yard to grow at will (by specifically not weeding, mowing, or using any herbicides or pesticides), several native species have Rewilded themselves, including native plants such as Oregon Ash / Rowan, Hazel, Western Red Cedar, Big Leaf Maple, and native Oaks. Just this year, Stinging Nettle finally established themselves wildly in the yard after us hoping for it for a long time. Keep in mind, I didn't *plant* any of the above. These are the plants and trees that just naturally came back when left alone. Reforestation is happening on its own.

There are a huge number of bird species and pollinator species that regularly live in or near my yard now, and raccoons and squirrels are frequent guests. My neighbors often quizzically wonder about the squirrels getting onto the roof or the raccoons visiting at night, but they seem quite content to eat the Blueberries, Acorns, and Hazelnuts without damaging the property in any way. We've also had snakes, lizards, owls, and even deer in our yard, and please keep in mind that we live in the middle of town quite far from the nearest forest park.

This approach is now taking off nationally and internationally as the Homegrown National Park (HNP) movement. The idea is that by Rewilding our yards, we can establish native habitats for plant and animal species that equal or exceed the space provided by national parks. People around the world are now looking at their backyard as natural wildlife refuges, and by establishing native plants, wild animals are returning and being nourished.

Rewilding Our Lives

Rewilding our lives so that we live and act more in harmony with the ecological systems around us and are deeply informed by our ancestral ways is really what this whole book is about. It is work I've been involved with for over thirty years, and as we mentioned in the "Reconnection" chapter, if it's a given that humans have been living as hunter-gatherer-gardener-nomads deeply immersed in nature for over 200,000 years, it's no wonder that we feel pretty disconnected from our current lives.

However, it's not realistic or practical to have us all abandon our modern day lives and suddenly try to live like hunter-gatherers. This would be devastating to the natural world (as we plunder already stressed ecosystems that can't handle our population and its impact) and devastating to humans (since many of us would have no idea what we would be doing). Rather, we can incorporate ancestral ways of living into our modern lives that nourish both us and the planet.

Here's a list of some of the ways of redesigning and Rewilding our lives that would likely make all of us healthier and happier:

- Foraging for wild foods
- Making our own herbal medicines
- Reestablishing a relationship with fire[20] (and wood)
- Knowing how to get our basic needs met from the natural world (learning realistic, practical, place-based survival skills)
- Spending more time outside in a nature-based environment and less time in a sedentary position looking at screens
- Building a food forest in our backyard, filled with fruit trees, native berry bushes, and wild greens
- Climbing trees, hiking/moving off trail, and exploring our inner animal forms of movement (see the "Rewilding as a Bard" section below for more details)
- Establishing an ethical relationship toward meat (if we choose to eat it) by hunting, fishing, or being involved with the procurement of it
- Learning to handmake functional items for our lives, including bowls, utensils, clothing, and more

Natural Rhythms and Rewilding

One of the biggest disconnections we face from our ancient ancestors, modern-day hunter-gatherers, and healthy nature-based cultures in general is a deep separation from the natural cycles and rhythms of nature. We are thrown off from daily and seasonal cycles in a big way, and restoring and reconnecting to these rhythms can be a vital part of Rewilding.

Perhaps the single biggest example of this is the completely modern and very capitalist notion that we should maintain the exact level of productivity and activity through the winter months as through the summertime. This is completely in opposition to nature and to nature-based cultures. In nature, winter is a time of dormancy, rest, and deep relaxation and is when we sleep more, eat the stores of food we have gathered, and work on projects as we sink deep into the wisdom of culture. Or at least that's how it is in some places, how it was, and how it could be.

Instead, winter (and in particular December) is a time of high intensity, with people rushing around shopping, still working full time, traveling extensively, and going to parties. Is it any wonder, then, that we are barraged with colds and the flu and then a month later find ourselves overwhelmed by the winter blues? There are some alternative-medicine doctors who are now putting forth the notion that seasonal affective disorder is simply a result of not allowing people to rest and rejuvenate enough, and a reflection of our own inability to accept dormancy and inwardness as natural states.

Of course, this extends to other seasons and to other rhythms as well. I'm pretty sure it was not part of our ancient ancestral rhythms to magically make an hour disappear every spring and then magically reappear in the fall. And now we are seeing the consequences of this seasonal adjustment of the clocks as stress goes up, concentration is affected, and both heart attacks and car accidents spike in the two weeks after daylight "saving" time goes into effect.

What are our options? Here's a list of ways to Rewild our natural rhythms:

- As often as possible, try to interact with and observe sunrise and sunset. This is perhaps the most ancient of natural rhythms.
- Observe the moon cycle (new, waxing, full, waning) and notice how you feel both physically and emotionally as the moon changes.
- Experience daylight and sunlight on your skin at least once a day.
- Go outside at night and observe the stars and moonlight multiple times a week.
- Track your feelings, emotions, and energy during each season and see if you can adjust your behavior accordingly (more activity in spring and summer, more rest and inward focus in fall and winter).

- Try to limit electronic light at night, especially screens. Try having candlelight or a fire at night at least once a week to reset your biological clock.
- Consider one evening by candlelight instead of modern lighting.
- Observe the major seasonal changes, such as spring equinox, fall equinox, solstices, etc.
- On some days, do away with clocks or timepieces and just observe the movement of the sun.
- Experiment with alternative time systems such as a sundial or no time at all.
- Create periods of time in your life that are fully free of scheduled items.
- Create periods of time where you can fully unplug and disconnect.

Story of the Present:

REWILDING BEGINS

In the first three decades of the twenty-first century, the biosphere continues to be eroded at an alarming rate across all species. Insects suddenly disappear, bird populations crash, and large herds of animals following their traditional migration routes become rarer and rarer. A full two-thirds of wild areas of the planet are now gone, leaving a scant one-third remaining, somewhat intact wild places existing within the biosphere.

And yet, something mysterious and wondrous is happening at the same time . . .

Wolves have been deliberately returned to the Greater Yellowstone Ecosystem and to southern Idaho. Their populations thrive, explode, spread to other areas, and actually restore whole ecosystems, leading to booms in grizzly bear populations, the return of ground-nesting bird species, and a healthful culling of elk populations. Wolves also repopulate other parts of the Lower 48 states in the US on their own, reestablishing themselves from wild Canadian populations. They also show up in eastern Europe on the outskirts of Berlin and thrive in the now-wild places all around Chernobyl.

Bison herds have reestablished and grown within the confines of Yellowstone National Park, while also spreading into their traditional territory through bison farms. As bison meat grows in popularity, bison actually displace cattle from open ranges throughout the Western United States. Native tribes such as the Cheyenne and Blackfoot are able to restore their own bison herds and have bison in their traditional territory for the first time in generations.

In the Pacific Northwest of North America, the Snoqualmie people have used massive casino revenue to buy back tens of thousands of acres of their traditional land. Their forest plan for the land is to "leave it alone." In addition, the Snoqualmie have established a cultural center at Snoqualmie Falls (a site of great cultural and spiritual significance for the tribe), regularly conduct public native plant restoration plantings for native salmon, and help reestablish a population of kokanee salmon, the "little red fish," in Lake Sammamish, the traditional breeding grounds for this threatened species.

Meanwhile, in the South Pacific, different island states experiment with implementing no-fishing zones to protect the local fish populations and traditional fishing practices. The zones are wildly successful, well beyond expectations, and fish populations in the no-fishing zones become so prolific they spill over in vast quantities into regular fishing areas. Fish populations are restored, traditional fishing is saved, and the overall ecological health of the area rebounds. A win for everyone.

Finally, around Chernobyl, where humans can no longer enter due to high levels of radioactivity, wildlife not seen for generations returns. Black grouse, Eurasian lynx, wolves, wild boar, moose, and beavers are present in unexpectedly high numbers able to exist even with the presence of radioactivity.

Deliberate Rewilding of the planet has begun in key areas . . . and it keeps spreading!

Rewilding as a Bard

GATHERING, CREATING, AND MOVEMENT

Human expression has become increasingly digital, to the point that visual artists, writers, and craftspeople literally can't support themselves in much of the world without a digital presence. As this book is being put together, AI programs are seriously threatening the work of visual artists as well as poets and storytellers. But once upon a time, story, song, dance, and art was a participatory practice done together around fires. What have we lost and what can we recover by Rewilding our arts and expression again?

Gathering Around the Fire

I have been startled several times when witnessing the reaction both in myself and others of the simple art of having people gather around a fire at night and sharing. In some sense, this should be no surprise, since for uncountable millennia this was the *only* form of "entertainment" available to everyone. And to describe the cultural exchange, wisdom, and transmission that took place as entertainment is to do it a true disservice.

Once upon a time, story, song, and dance (often in the evening, around the fire) were some of the primary means not only of artistic expression, but also of sharing deep wisdom, teachings, and knowledge inherent in culture. People became animals and mythological characters and reenacted primal stories answering the biggest questions of our existence, such as where do we come from, why are we here, and what are we supposed to do.

Elaborate handmade costumes crafted with materials directly gathered from the local bioregion allowed people to make these transformations and bring a living, magical element to the gatherings.

How do we recapture and rebuild this magic? Well, it might not be as hard as we think, and the truth of the matter is that it might already be happening.

It is no surprise that in the twenty-first century, an eruption of popularity of music, culture, and arts festivals has exploded around the globe, made most famous of course by the spark that ignited this movement: Burning Man. It is no coincidence that people now gather from all walks of life, wear incredibly creative and elaborate costumes, and dance to music outside for days on end. I believe that this cultural explosion is directly tied to the emptiness of our daily lives and mainstream culture. The longing to be outside with other humans and creatively express ourselves is so powerful that is has now become a global movement of outdoor musical and cultural festivals taking place in many different countries. But what about when we aren't at the music festivals, or what about the people for whom that isn't their scene?

It is quite common at festivals and gatherings of all sorts for people to once again gather around a fire and share song, stories, and dance underneath the stars and get in touch with the ancient, wild part of themselves that once did that regularly. In fact, the nurturing, fulfilling feeling that people gain from gathering with others around a fire through song, story, and dance was once the *nightly* routine for people everywhere, and for Indigenous people around the globe, undistracted by the glamour of modern technology, these gatherings are still happening.

A little bit more wild and nourishing than Netflix and chill! It doesn't take much to gather with a group of friends or people of like mind and make a fire in someone's backyard to share stories, song, and fun. Specifically, make this a practice of taking a break from screens and devices for all involved. Do it at least once a month and you might be startled at what happens to those people and their connection to each other and the world around them.

Rewilding Our Art

It was not that long ago, perhaps a couple of hundred years ago, when *all* art, including paintings, sculptures, drawings, and handmade items such as baskets, were completely crafted not only by hand but with all-natural materials foraged from the local ecosystem. Pigments, paints, and inks were crafted out of a wide variety of plant, animal, and fungal products, which required a deep, rich relationship with the local ecosystem. Sculptures were created with handmade tools or our hands and used materials such as wood, stone, or clay that was gathered by humans. The vast industrialization of the world has changed many of these relationships dramatically, resulting in mass-produced, cheap, plastic goods often made with toxic materials and ingredients. And now, a lot of our art has become digital and even virtual, reaching a point of absurdity with the advent of AI.

Digital art is perhaps one of the best examples of how human arts is an inherent part of our culture, which we will bring with us to all mediums. It has its own beauty and value that certainly expresses human creativity and culture. However, it is definitely a very different expression of our artistic impulse than the very tangible expressions found in ancient rock art, handmade and decorated pottery, and handwoven baskets.

It is also important to note that in many ancient cultures, as well as in living Indigenous cultures, the separation between durable, useful, everyday goods and items from art is not present to the same extent as in our modern, highly technological world. Artistic expression and flair was often a part of items such as baskets, footwear, clothing, jewelry, and tools (including weapons)—this is the art of the "folk," or functional, everyday art. Much of this was (and in some cases still is) highly individualistic but also expressive of deep cultural teachings and truths. Bows painted with ancient symbols, baskets woven with stories into their warp and weft, and boomerangs with cultural teachings embedded in their surface are just a few examples. Contrast this with the proliferation of cheap plastic goods that saturate meaning of our own homes and lives.

While it may seem daunting and probably perplexing to undertake Rewilding our art, you might be surprised at how incredibly *satisfying* it is to make something by hand. Learning to dig clay from the earth and make a simple cup or bowl, taking classes on natural basket weaving, and learning to gather our own natural paints and pigments are just a few examples of how to dive into this world.

One thing you might do is learn how to forage for local basketry materials and try your hand at making baskets. These baskets may be foraged from vines (including many that threaten ecosystems, such as Kudzu, Bittersweet, Buckthorn, and Honeysuckle vine—all problematic in many ecosystems in North America). You can also learn to grow gourds and make baskets with those materials, pine needles, daffodil stems, and much more.

A second wonderful way to learn the art around you is to learn how to carve or work with wood. A simple set of carving tools can open up the worlds of functional wooden art—spoon carving, bowl carving, walking sticks, handles, and many other wonderful things can be made from the wood outside your door. Woodturning offers yet another possibility to work with local woods. Another thing you can do is saw simple thin rounds from branches approximately 1½–3 inches across and use a woodburner tool to burn various designs—make pendants, tree ornaments, garden planting markers, and much more.

Another area that is growing within the Rewilding art movement is learning how to make your own paints and pigments from your local landscape. This involves going out and looking for clay deposits, pigments that you can find on the land, or soft stones, or using plant-based dyes. When a stone is rubbed on a rock, look to see what pigment it leaves behind. These stones can be carefully ground (using a mask to avoid breathing rock dust) to a fine powder and then sifted with a fine strainer. Add a bit of honey and gum arabic (or another local tree gum) and mix these together. Pour into a shell, nutshell, or carved-out piece of wood, and then you will have a local watercolor paint, which you can wet and use. If you find several different pigments to work with, you will eventually create an entire local palette!

A final area that is wonderful for rewilding and art is to learn some ancient pottery methods. Begin by finding a local clay bank and dig clay. Depending on the quality of the clay, you may have to do some initial processing, which would involve soaking the clay and then straining it through a screen to ensure it is more pure and ready to work with. Shape your clay into whatever you want (making sure it is not more than ¾ inch thick—thicker clay can explode if an air bubble is trapped inside). Let your clay dry completely. Then you can build a natural "kiln," which is basically just a large bonfire. Your clay pieces are in the center of the fire; you build a wooden "box" around them and then make a giant fire with brush and other natural materials. Light the fire, letting it burn down naturally without adding much wood or tending it. In the morning, sift through the ashes to find your natural clay pieces.

Rewilding Our Bodies

When we speak of domestication and of the desire to Rewild, it is necessary to also look at how, where, when, and in what ways we move our bodies. Every day, more and more research is showing how our sedentary lifestyle is at the root of so many of our health problems (including obesity, diabetes, heart disease, and depression). Yet, for many people the idea of going to a gym and moving on treadmills or lifting metallic weights in various ways, shapes, and forms just isn't appealing. Let me explain why.

First of all, exercise is actually a fairly modern concept. In many traditional societies, movement, strength training, and mobility were built into everyday life. The modern push to get in ten thousand steps is probably related to the fact that as hunter-gatherer-nomads, we moved around a significant amount every day. Hunting, gathering, gardening, and making everything takes work, and it's not just a dull repetitious movement done over and over. Climbing trees, digging roots, chasing animals, throwing spears, shooting bows, making fire, weaving a basket, and so forth all require dynamic, multidimensional physical effort.

Contrast that with what we currently do in a day: driving a car for forty to sixty minutes every morning, sitting in an office with only minimal breaks while staring at a screen all day and making minor movements with your fingers, then eating lunch, more of the same in the afternoon, then a similar commute home, possibly some intensive sudden exercise, and more screen time at night.

Or, to use another lens, imagine looking at, moving, and interacting with only flat, two-dimensional shapes all day, every day. Compare and contrast this with just the complexity of what it takes to climb and play in a tree for five to ten minutes!

Our bodies crave and desire time outside in nature, moving in sophisticated and complex ways. And primal movement, natural movement, rewilding our bodies, and other forms of moving naturally, especially outside, have taken off in the last decade, transforming the fitness industry.

Rewilding our bodies is a process unto itself and could easily form a book on its own, but here are several simple ways to Rewild and rebuild your body by tapping into its inherent desire to move and be outside in a natural, free way:

- Hiking, walking, trail running, and exploring nature, especially off-trail (if you can find an ecologically responsible way)
- Swimming in wild water such as rivers, lakes, or the ocean (be sure to be safe!)
- Climbing a tree (you don't even have to go high; a few feet off the ground is entirely magical for many folks)
- Lifting rocks, logs, and other heavy natural objects
- Making things out of nature (stone tools, fire kits, fire making, gathering basket materials and making baskets)
- Playing games with friends outside (epic adult game of capture the flag, anyone?)
- Moving on all fours (quadrupedal movement) or moving like animals
- Yoga, tai chi, martial arts, and other movement-based systems done outside, immersed in the natural elements
- Winter sports such as snowshoeing, skiing, ice-skating, and more (learn to build your own snowshoes out of local materials!)

- Dancing around a fire at night with friends and live drummers
- Homesteading and gardening practices, a lifestyle that requires everyday physical movement as you tend animals, plants, and the earth around you

Even for those with limited mobility or disability, you can still find a way to move—even if it's just a small part of your body. Play music and dance with your head and hands, use your toes and feet to mimic the movement of fish, or place your hands in a running stream.

As you can see, Rewilding our bodies is an endless journey combining our natural impulses and instincts, the outdoors, creativity, and the simple practice of moving our body in all the ways it doesn't move in a sedentary lifestyle!

Rewilding as a Druid
OFFERINGS, CEREMONIES, AND PRACTICES

Rewilding our spirituality, ceremonies, and meditation is probably the work of many generations, but it's important to note that even many of the famous teachers and prophets of major world religions had their most profound spiritual revelations outside. Buddha achieved enlightenment under a tree at dawn, Jesus spent forty days and nights in the desert, and Moses received a revelation from God through a burning bush.

Learning to meditate outside, doing ceremony outside, and Rewilding our cosmology are just a few steps toward Rewilding as seen through the Druid lens.

As we began to explore in chapters 1 and 2, when people deepen their relationship to nature and internalize and embody the ecology of their bioregion, amazing things start to occur. For many, they start to have spontaneous spiritual experiences in nature, including (but certainly not limited to) a sense of oneness with all things, a natural quieting of their mind and even extinguishing of thought, and a deep sense that different beings and elements are trying to communicate with them. In some sense, the closer we grow to a place, including its natural rhythms, and the more we form an intimate relationship with the trees, plants, birds, mammals, rocks, fungi, and so on, the more we connect to and unveil the *spirit* of a place. Dozens of people I know have found themselves falling into a natural form of animism as they go on a journey of nature spirituality. We discussed this extensively in the last chapter, on Respect, but it is helpful to mention it again as part of Rewilding our spirituality and to review a few key points.

Rewilding Our Offerings

As we began to explore in chapter 2, "Respect," one of the ways that people have classically established and grown relationships with the unseen (including ancestors, nature spirits, deities, gods/goddesses, and more) has been through the practice of making offerings. You can find this in all of the world's major religions, and today it is kept alive in such practices as diverse as monks making incense offerings placed on altars in temples, to shamans making offerings directly to the land to nurture wild spirits. These offerings are often conceived of as gifts that establish and maintain relationships between humans and spiritual forces, with the benefit extending to all.

What does making offerings have to do with Rewilding? And what would Rewilded offerings look like? Well, consider for a moment the idea that there was a time (and there are still places) when people continually made offerings to the local bioregion where they lived. This was done at various times, including in general, throughout the year, when there was a special occasion, when someone really needed something from nature, and especially when something was taken from nature. Now imagine that these offerings would go to the local nature spirits, nourishing them and causing the land and all of its inhabitants to thrive. What would happen if this was done continually for hundreds or even thousands of years? The traditional teaching around this is that the land, the biosphere, *and* the humans all would thrive, being mutually nourished.

Now imagine the opposite: humans taking from nature all the time, with no offering of even the merest gratitude. What might happen to humans, the nature spirits, and the biosphere? Probably what we're seeing currently on a global scale: massive disruption of the biosphere, widespread loss of species, and a prevalence of instability and mental health issues in humans.

This is not to suggest that making offerings to our local nature spirits is suddenly going to reverse global climate change (though we don't know that it won't help reverse the process). However, what is being suggested is that solely relying on human material cultural changes might not be the only thing we need to do to Rewild the planet. Undertaking the practice of making offerings will look different to everyone, but here are some ways that people have traditionally made offerings to nature spirits and the animate world around them:

- Sprinkling cornmeal, tobacco, or another plant substance as an offering to the earth and other unseen powers
- Offering water to plants and trees, especially before harvesting or gathering from them
- Singing to the trees, plants, rivers, lakes, oceans, and other features of your bioregion
- Remembering all the nonhuman world in your prayers and praying for their healing and rejuvenation (praying for the trees, plants, animals, rocks, and so forth)
- Offering something beautiful and handmade to the earth or waters
- Traditionally in Europe, offerings of sweet baked goods and dairy were made to the Fae folk and nature spirits.
- Burning herbs, incense, or other pleasant-smelling items on or near fire
- Asking the land for what it wants or needs as an offering (and listening deeply to its answer)

As we deepen our exploration of offerings here, consider that rewilded offerings may be one of the most powerful and direct ways we can "feed" the earth, our bioregion, and its local inhabitants for the benefit of nature *and* humans. Also, consider for a moment that it's probably been quite some time since your local bioregion was fed in this way; in fact, it could be starving. You can be the difference between starvation and substance, for such a little bit of time and energy.

Cosmology: Genius Loci

As we deepen our relationship to place and go on a journey with the interconnectivity of nature, humans, and spirits, not only is it common for an animist worldview to emerge, but we may also find ourselves connecting with very specific kinds of spiritual forces. One of the most common experiences on this path is to connect with the actual spirit of a place. Known as the genius loci (literally, Greek for spirit of a specific place and etymologically related to the word "djinn" or "genie"), the personification of a particular is an ancient recognized magical relationship.

Of course, which place can become a relevant question. But it is totally possible to develop a relationship with a very large, bioregionally significant natural feature. For instance, in the Pacific Northwest of North America, there are very large volcanic peaks in the Cascades that dominate the local landscape. Traditionally, they all were seen as having specific spirits and personalities and being full of potent spiritual energy. This includes the largest mountain around, known as Tahoma (also known as Mount Rainier and many other local names), and the well-known, very volcanically active Lewitt (known as Mount St. Helens to many). But the genius loci that you connect with may be significantly smaller or larger than what I've described.

Again, speaking of the Pacific Northwest, there is definitely a spiritual presence in the valley I live in, known as the Snoqualmie Valley. Snoqualmie is also the tribal name of the local caretakers and traditional people of the land. It is also the name of the main river system of the area, and there is a major waterfall of deep spiritual significance along the river, known as Snoqualmie Falls. All of these become interconnected when you realize that the word "Snoqualmie" is related to the moon, and the moon is personified in local stories as a powerful, changer spirit who made all the natural features of the area.

Finally, this understanding can apply to other areas, including cities or whole bioregions. There is definitely a specific spirit that I have come to know, associated with the city of Seattle, and Cascadia is a perfect name for both the bioregion I live in *and* the spirit of the bioregion. Learning to reach out, connect with, and make offerings to the spirits of the place and places you are in is a powerful way to Rewild our spiritual path.

Rewilding Our Meditation

Meditative practices are key parts of many spiritual traditions. In chapter 1, we looked at how sitting outside in nature all alone may be the original form of human meditation. This key practice is still a wonderful core practice of nature spirituality, but there are other ways to Rewild our meditation and points to consider. Is it more natural to meditate inside or outside? What ways can we bring nature into our meditation practice? What are the oldest, most-ancient forms of meditation, and how can they inform any meditation we do in the present?

A rewilded meditation practice is one that is best done outside in nature when possible, and meditative forms can arise organically rather than be prescribed or stuffy. It is not about sitting still and closing yourself off from the world, but, rather, opening yourself up fully to nature to be present in the here and now.

- Visualizing yourself as a tree with roots extended deep into the earth and branches extended up into the sky (this can be done seated or standing)
- Meditating outside at various times and places, including in the sunlight; under the moonlight; near rivers, mountains, or deserts; and under trees in the forest
- Practicing moving meditation, especially a form of movement in which you take on the form of an animal or natural element, including tai chi, internal martial arts, yoga, hula, and other forms of traditional dance
- Build a fire outside with materials you have gathered yourself (and if you can, start it with an ancient method). Quietly sit and tend the fire by yourself for an extended period of time (at least an hour and up to several hours) and notice what happens to your mind and senses.
- Practice visualizing your body as made up of the natural elements around you, including earth, weather, fire, air, and spirit.
- Visualizing the inside of the body as an inner landscape that mirrors the outer landscape
- Meditating with different aspects or elements of nature, including mountains, rivers, rock formations, deserts, lakes, or oceans
- Meditating with trees, plants, and fungi
- Sitting still in nature and deeply listening to the birds and what they are saying

Rewilding Our Ceremonies

One of the main things I have heard from people over the years about why nature is spiritual for them is simply the idea that they feel as though *being outside is more spiritual than inside.* For many folks, the best churches, the most-beautiful cathedrals, and the most-magnificent temples are found in nature itself in the form of mountains, old-growth trees, red-rock deserts, ocean overlooks, and majestic waterfalls. In fact, there is a compelling argument that the most-magnificent churches, cathedrals, and temples are actually based on patterns in nature and deliberately mimic the feelings invoked in a place such as old-growth forests (this is particularly true of the design of medieval cathedrals in Europe).

No one can say for sure when or how people began doing ceremonies, but it is a key component of the relationships among humans, nature, and spirit. Also, it's important to realize that while having scripted, deliberate ceremonies can work and does work for some, *there is a place and space where all ceremony comes from.* It is my belief that ceremony is birthed at the intersection of humans, nature, and spirit and is found in wild, natural places. Not only that, but once upon a time, all of our ceremonies were conducted with handmade materials, harvested in a respectful manner, and used to unify, harmonize, and rejuvenate humans, nature, and the unseen. Rewilding our ceremonies is a key part of Rewilding our relationship with nature and spirit.

But how can we do this in the complex world of the twenty-first century? Here are some suggestions:

- Conducting ceremony outside in a natural setting, even if that's a backyard or a city park
- Including the natural world and all of nature's elements in the scope of our ceremony, including trees, plants, animals, fungi, rocks, land features, and more. This means that rather than bringing ritual tools into a space, use the space and aspects of nature as your tools.
- Using natural handmade items in our ceremony, including but not limited to herb bundles wild-crafted in a sacred manner, pouches or satchels made and decorated by hand with natural pigments and dyes, and wearing ceremonial garb we have helped create with our hands and with natural materials
- Following natural rhythms and rewilded time schedule to conduct ceremony at the liminal times such as dusk and dawn, and celestially significant time such as following moon cycles and solstices and equinoxes
- Finding natural, sacred places in wild nature that call out for ceremony

- Building natural altars out of the earth itself and using found materials, including rocks, sticks, feathers, plant material, and bones, to create the altar (making sure not to disrupt the ecosystem in this process)
- Building our ceremonial tools out of natural material we gather by hand, including wands and staff made from downed trees or branches and stones and rocks we find in the wild

As we began exploring in chapter 1, it can be downright intimidating to perform a ceremony, and it might be helpful to have some simple guidelines if you are new to it. As we already explored, ceremonies don't have to be formal or scripted, and a rewilded approach to ceremony can be extremely powerful, since there is no right or wrong thing to do. Just flow with what your intuition tells you and what the land provides. Here are some additional ideas:

- Often, ceremonies have a clear *opening* or start. This can involve invoking protection, creating a defined space, and some form of purification such as with ceremonial smoke.
- Usually during a ceremony, it is helpful to drop into ceremonial space or consciousness with a form of grounding or meditation.
- After everyone is present and grounded, stating the big-picture intention for the ceremony is usually helpful.
- Calling in spiritual forces that are a part of the ceremony often happens next.
- Making offerings to the spirits and nature is key.
- Sharing specific intentions and prayers, especially from individuals, is helpful.
- Singing songs, making music, and dancing all can be a part of or the main focus of the ceremony.
- Wrapping up with either big-picture sharing or individual sharing is also important.
- A formal closing and releasing of spiritual forces is essential.

- Leaving the sacred space and stepping back into normal time and space wraps up the ceremony for everyone.

This is a rough outline, and while some people are very particular about the parameters of ceremony, it is important to remember that people have been creating ceremony since our earliest times on this planet. It is your birthright and an essential part of being human. You have what it takes to birth, create, and design ceremonies that Rewild our relationship with nature. And if you are wondering what kind of ceremony can be Rewilded, here are few examples that can be done solo or with a group of people:

- A simple gratitude ceremony for all the elements and beings in your bioregion, done by yourself or others
- A ceremony of rejuvenation and regeneration (including making offerings) for the nature spirits and the natural world around you. The focus of this ceremony is to heal, nourish, and rejuvenate the land by giving back.
- Outdoor ceremonies performed under the full moon
- Ceremonies held at significant sun cycles, including equinox, solstices, and possibly in between
- Blessings and offerings for special natural features near you, including rivers, the ocean, waterfalls, other waterways, large trees, mountains, or special rock features. Again, this is a great practice to do solo or with a group.
- Any sort of land-healing ceremony, especially done for places where there has been ecological damage or destruction (important to work *with* the local spirits here, including asking them if they want to have healing and what form that might take). More on this in chapter 6, "Reenchantment."

Story of the Future:

A REWILDED WORLD

Through careful and thoughtful designation of 50 percent of the Earth's surface and ocean as wilderness, natural systems have been restored, animal species have rebounded, the oceans are prolific, and the global climate has stabilized. Vast herds of large animals make their annual migrations across several different continents, and populations of reindeer, caribou, wildebeest, bison, elk, and others are now fulfilling their natural role in ecosystem transformation and regulation. Large and small predators have been reintroduced or have rebounded as well, and the biodiversity and biomass of wild animals are at a level not seen for centuries.

Cities are kept cool and moderate, with a plethora of green rooftops, urban food forests, and wild green corridors, allowing their inhabitants plenty of time for urban forest bathing and rejuvenation practices while living in a regenerative urban environment. Food is grown on rooftops in the cities and throughout suburban homesteads in the form of yardens and food forests that surround the city, providing backyard wildlife sanctuaries and supplementary local organic food and herbal medicines. Farms have been reimagined with little or no tilling and as integrated wild areas. Large animals including bison and cattle are intelligently integrated into farm plans, as are local wildlife.

Indigenous tribes are at the head of regional efforts to restore and rejuvenate local animal populations and bioregions. Wealth is now seen as a collective process and includes the local ecological populations thriving as a true indicator of prosperity. Ceremonies are conducted on a rhythmic basis daily, monthly, and in accordance with the sun to harmonize the relationship among nature, humanity, and the spirit world. All three thrive in balance and harmony, and people's lives include ample time in nature, using their hands and participating in their own food and health. There is also plenty of time for artistic expression both individually and collectively, as people gather around fires to share stories, dance, and make music in celebration of life.

The world has been rewilded.

BARD
Regenerating relationships with self & community
DRUID
Ceremonies of Land regeneration
The microcosm & macrocosm
OVATE
Regenerating ecosystems & Land stewardship
Regrowing
Repair
Healing
Replanting
REGENERATION

CHAPTER 4

Regeneration

With Dana O'Driscoll

Story of the Past:

SULPHUR CREEK

The Allegheny Mountains in western Pennsylvania were once some of the most diverse ecosystems in the world. The peoples there—the Shawnee, Susquehannock, Osage, Massamoweck, Manahoac, Monacan—cultivated abundant food forests full of nuts, fruits, and medicines; had clear streams and rivers brimming with bass and trout; and tended the land so that all would thrive. One such clean and beautiful creek, whose previous name is lost, ran through the Allegheny Mountains. Full of fish, crayfish, mussels, and more, the creek was a welcome source of nourishment and clean water for humans and all life in the area.

Then the settlers came. With colonization came an insatiable greed for the resources of the land; this greed paved the way for industrialization. As these lands suffered under their new human inhabitants, nearly 98 percent of the forests were cut, seams of bituminous and anthracite coal were opened from the body of the earth, and runoff from the mines and steel mills poisoned the waterways.

Our clean and beautiful creek suffered this fate. The creek grew acidic and polluted, a bright-orange color, full of what is now called AMD, acid mine drainage. Long after mining ends, the mines continue to emit polluted water and the pollution remains with the community, enduring, taking root, and making the streams lifeless. Sometimes, this AMD can last for hundreds or even thousands of years.

Now a century after the industrial boom ended, the people of the Allegheny Mountains live in the remnants of this scarred yet slowly healing landscape. In Pennsylvania at the end of the twentieth century, over 3,000 miles of streams had severe acid mine drainage, rendering the waterways lifeless. Like so many others, our creek has been flowing with extreme pollution for over a hundred years. The creek has now been named for the color and the smell, "Sulphur Creek"—this is the name that is on the maps and in the hearts and minds of the inhabitants.

INTRODUCING REGENERATION

The story above is a very personal story, a story of my own settler ancestors and the place where I grew up, and yet, something like this is part of the lived experiences of so many human beings today. What does it mean to live next to a river that is full of poison? What does it mean to live near a mountain that has been removed? Or to live near a toxic dump, or even in suburbia, where countless sprays, mowers, and pesticides continually damage nature and prevent life from flourishing? The truth is that right now, seeing damaged ecosystems, living in polluted areas, or witnessing firsthand the repeated destruction of nature is commonplace. What are the effects of these polluted places on our communities? Why do the poorest of communities always have the worst toxic and environmental issues? And why are those same communities often broken and hurting? How do we even begin—as individuals and as a community—to heal a river that has been poisoned for over a century?

These questions form the crux of one of the many challenges we face as humans living in this age: what to do about the legacy of damage, the ongoing destruction of the planet, and the degradation of our relationships with each other. I believe that damaged ecosystems work on the subconscious. Just as our ecosystem is degraded, so too are we damaged. As we heal our ecosystems, we heal our communities and ourselves and bring hope back. And this, my friends, is why regeneration matters!

Regeneration means to regrow, heal, restore, or return what was lost. When we regenerate, we work with nature's systems to heal ourselves, each other, our communities, and our world. As Robin Wall Kimmerer notes in *Braiding Sweetgrass*, "It is not enough to weep for our lost landscapes; we have to put our hands in the earth to make ourselves whole again" (p. 347).

As we explore in this chapter, Regeneration is rooted in four key principles:

- The ability of nature and nature's systems to repair and heal damage; this is literally what nature does best when given the opportunity.
- The ability of humans to support those natural cycles and healing and be a force of good
- The ability of humans to regenerate relationships with themselves, each other, and nature
- The importance of care as a foundation for all regeneration

One of the things that the Sit Spot practice in chapter 1 can teach us over time is the power of nature's cycles to heal and repair the landscape. A large branch falls from a tree, and you will observe that within a few months' time, it is quickly covered in mushrooms. These mushrooms break down the lignin or cellulose; insects burrow inside, moss covers the branch, and in a few short years, the wood turns into soil, where new things grow. Observing the natural world shows you any number of nature's systems that are breaking down, clearing, purifying, and regrowing. This is the healing power of nature—and since humans are also part of nature, we can be a part of nature's healing system: scattering seeds, planting trees, and even rebuilding our communities.

Ultimately, the work of regeneration is the work of care. Modern life doesn't leave a lot of room for care. In fact, it is pretty much the opposite: Modern industrial society values efficiency and economic growth at all costs—and these values create systems that are cold, hard, and inflexible. These values are what has gotten us into the mess we are all facing now, and these values are what continue to harm all life on this planet. What is missing is care: caring for each other, caring for nature, caring for the future, and caring for ourselves. Regeneration is caring enough to offer healing and hope, even when it is difficult to do so. As you do this regenerative work, go with love into your community, into your garden, into your forest, into whatever spaces and places call for you. As Kimmerer notes in *Braiding Sweetgrass*, "Restoration is a powerful antidote to despair" (p. 328). By focusing on healing damaged places, people, and communities, we offer a powerful vision of hope.

Regeneration allows us to write a new story for the present and future. It allows us to learn how to reindigenize to our local place, to spiritually and physically root in a place that we tend and care for. Our triad of practices in this chapter starts with the physical regeneration of our lands and ecosystems through Ovate work. Physical regeneration of the land is necessary work if life is to survive on this planet, because so many ecosystems have been degraded or destroyed by human activity. Regeneration of our ecosystems and lands allows us to take collective and personal responsibility for what our species has done to the planet in the last few centuries. Most importantly, regeneration reorients our relationship to the land as caretakers and care-filled beings. While the land has been degraded and damaged, so have our communities and social structures. Thus, the second strand of the braid of regeneration, the path of the Bard, helps us rebuild and re-form our relationships to each other and to ourselves—recognizing the need for us to care for each other. The third strand is the path of the Druid, where we recognize the importance of people coming together to do ceremonies on behalf of all life, for the earth, for ourselves, and for our collective future.

This threefold philosophy of regeneration offers each of us a path into healing our earth—and that work might be different depending on who you are, where you live, and what your strengths are. And that's okay! We all are different, and yet, we all have something to offer. The most important thing is that we all work to do something—not look away, not just despair, but act for the good of all.

And these three strands are deeply interwoven: Regenerating our communities will help rekindle the tribal bonds that hold us together, encourage us to engage in local action and address local challenges, and also allow us to collectively rebuild our relationship with the land. This work is also absolutely critical to ensure that future generations born into our communities have a strong and stable place to grow. Personal regeneration is necessary for all of this, because if you are broken, you cannot heal anyone or anything else. Finally, ceremonial work is necessary to do any outer work and support everything that we do in the physical world to make change. As we weave these three strands of the braid together, consider their interconnection. Consider how rebuilding strong communities supports strong individuals, who then can go into the world and create powerful change.

Perhaps it is easy to think about all that is going wrong and say, What can I possibly do? This is one more cultural narrative that is worthy of interrogation—the narrative that says we are powerless, that we should let those in authority solve the world's problems, and that all we can do is wait for them to do something. But the truth is, every one of us is in a local ecosystem directly connected to the living earth! Each one of us has the power to practice regeneration on our landscapes in powerful ways that make a difference for the life and people (nonhuman and human) outside our door. Removing ourselves from the equation, thinking that someone more powerful or knowledgeable should act, disempowers us and disconnects us.

Think, instead, of each of us as an interconnected tapestry. As though millions of individual humans, working regeneratively and with care in their hearts, are creating a web of stars that fill the sky. Suddenly those lights are everywhere, and nature is being healed on a large-scale level. Understand that you can make a difference in so many ways, and each of those ways matters. They matter to the birds that live in the tree in your backyard, they matter to the insect life that comes to the flowers growing in pots on your city windowsill, they matter to the flock of geese at your local pond, and they matter to the forest full of life that your community works to save.

Taking on a regenerative mindset is about shifting from a place of disempowerment to empowerment. It is about saying, "I can make a difference" and believing that to be true!

A regenerative mindset is both empowering and critically necessary for the coming age. It allows us to craft that vision and heal. It is this direct regeneration of our planet that holds, perhaps, the best hope for the future.

Regeneration as an Ovate
LAWNS, YARDENS, AND LAND STEWARDSHIP

Humans have a collective responsibility to tend, support, and bring the land back into healthy abundance. For one, we've created most of the problems we face, and for two, as we mentioned in the introduction, as Tyson Yunkaporta notes in *Sand Talk*, humans are the custodial species of the earth, and we are at our best when we are providing healing and support. While nature is capable of healing on her own (see chapter 3, "Rewilding"), given the current challenges, it is also critical that humans become a force of healing and good in this world and reestablish caretaking relationships with nature. That's what regeneration as an Ovate is all about—healing the land. We could fill a whole book with ideas on how to regenerate the landscape (and in fact, many people have, although they have not used our framework). Pick up any text on permaculture design, habitat restoration, or conservation and see what we mean (or see Dana's *Land Healing: Physical, Metaphysical, and Ritual Approaches to Healing the Earth*!). So, while we will offer a few very impactful techniques in this chapter, what also we hope to offer here is empowerment and vision.

Let's start with some general principles and philosophies to help us begin to think about how we would regenerate the natural world. These principles are adapted from permaculture design, a regenerative design system developed in the 1970s that helps humans work with nature to bring healing and abundance back to damaged land.

- **Observe and interact**. Get to know your land deeply. Work to identify what and who already lives on your land—is there something that might be endangered or at risk? By observing over a period of time and learning, you can figure out how to target your efforts. If you live in an area with a multitude of ecosystems, learn about them and spend time in them. If you live in an area that is devoid of most life (e.g., covered in lawn), you might be able to get started more quickly!

- **Work small, slow, and locally**. Learn about a specific plant, bird, fish, reptile, mammal, or insect and what you can do to promote its habitat and restoration. Take your time in understanding the needs and what you can do to support habitat restoration over time. Build a new habitat and expand that habitat over time.

- **Consider stacking functions**. Consider how you might carefully get many "yields" out of a single plant or space and maximize their benefits. For example, Common Milkweed (*Asclepias syriaca*) offers a range of benefits: Milkweed is a nectary and food source for a variety of butterflies, moths, and other insects; she is a nectary source for bees; she is beautiful and fun to observe; and she offers four different harvests for humans. If you want to create a meditation garden, consider how you might build it to suit not only you, but everything else that lives where you do—with lots of Milkweed!

- **Consider how you can do the most good**. Focus your energies on places, species, or building habitat in a way that offers the most impact in the region where you live. This will require you to seek out knowledge and build your own skill set so that you can heal the land. Learn what a healed local ecosystem looks like in terms of plants and life, and see what you can do to help bring your own ecosystem a few steps closer.

- **Collaborate with others**. Find other people who are also working to practice regeneration in your community and get involved. Learn from them. Many hands make light work!

- **Consider the future**. Good design does not think just about today or tomorrow, but ten, twenty, or even fifty years from now. Consider how things you might plant will grow and change over time, but also the role that a changing climate may have in your decisions.

While you might be tempted to start doing something immediately, a period of reflection, knowledge building, and interaction is key to regenerative work. It takes time to understand an ecosystem that exists, what an ecosystem might benefit from, and how you can best proceed in a way that maximizes the impact that you can make.

Now that we have a sense of some of the general principles for Regeneration, let's look at some specific roles you might take. These specific roles are intended to get you thinking about what you can do, your strengths and limitations, and how you might do good. We offer three roles here and note that two additional regenerative roles are discussed elsewhere in this book: the rewilder (chapter 3) and the refugium builder (chapter 5).

The Urban Gardener

Urban areas have been growing in size by about 1 million acres annually, displacing most other living beings in favor of concrete and human needs. I'm sure that anyone who has lived in an area can see the "new developments" springing up—most modern construction is nothing short of biological annihilation. The construction usually begins by stripping all life, even the topsoil (which becomes bagged and sold at home improvement stores) from the site where they are building. They then replace that life with buildings and concrete.

If you are one of the many people who live in an urban or suburban area (both in the United States and Europe, this is four in every five people), consider how you might cultivate mini refugia or an urban garden in your city or backyard. As the new paradigm takes shape, many cities have been experiencing a renaissance in community gardens, rooftop gardens, and other cultivated spaces. Urban settings offer unique challenges but also unique opportunities, especially to work in a community to cultivate intensively grown community gardens, rain gardens, urban beekeeping, guerrilla grafting on fruit trees lining city streets, rewilding abandoned areas, and much more. This is important work to do to allow life that is not human to still thrive and live in urban and suburban spaces. Think about how you can create spaces for other kinds of life beyond humans in the places where you live and work.

Start by taking a small area, even a few square feet, and observing that area for sunlight, rainfall, and other factors that may have an impact on plant growth. Choose one or more native species and intersperse them with some veggies or herbs if you'd like, observing and interacting with them. Observe the life that happens, enjoy the space, and keep expanding your growing garden. I will note that some of the most successful examples of this are in abandoned places (under bridges, near highways, etc.) in city environments.

You can find so many community gardens—often in urban areas—and they are worth seeking out and visiting. I have visited these all over the United States and beyond; what strikes me most is that each community garden has a unique character. While they often share similar features, no two are alike. Consider making it a point to visit as many as possible as you think about starting or joining an urban-gardening initiative!

The Yarden Advocate

Closely tied to the work of the urban gardener is the yarden advocate, which is a role that is best for people who live on lawn-dominated land in suburban or rural areas. In fact, the largest "crop" in many industrialized nations is the lawn. In the United States, lawns are the largest irrigated crop and take up around 40,000,000 acres or 50,000 square miles. The average yard size in the US is just over a ¼ acre (10,000 square feet), and lawns consume an average of 26 billion gallons of water annually (about 30 percent of the usage of water in the US). Lawns, at present, have displaced billions of acres of forests and other natural ecosystems, and inviting life "back in" through regenerative practices is a wonderful way to begin to shift the balance. Many lawns are also sprayed more heavily with pesticides, weed killers, and fertilizers than most conventionally produced foods and demand regular fossil fuel maintenance. Not to mention that most people find it a chore to maintain the lawn—who wants to mow grass on a hot summer day? All in all, these statistics represent how unsustainable the lawn is, and give motivation for a wonderful opportunity for change.

The term "yarden" is a hybrid of "yard + garden," and the term has been understood as meaning to convert lawns into spaces that produce an abundance of food for all life (including human life). Converting lawns into gardens, meadows, bee and butterfly sanctuaries, or refugia is an extremely important regenerative act. First, you are making more-ethical decisions about how you will tend and honor the land where you live and where you have the most impact. Second, you are rejecting the modern notion of lawns and lawn maintenance (which have steep ecological tolls) and seeking a more healthful relationship with the land where you live. Third, you are modeling an alternative path for others.

One of my best friends, Linda Jackson, runs Nature's Harvest Urban Farm on a quiet suburban street just north of Detroit, Michigan. What she found in the last seven years of cultivating her front-yard 50-by-50-foot garden is that if you create a yarden that is beautiful and looks like a unique landscape, the community will embrace the effort. Thus, while she is able to create habitat and grow vegetables in her landscaped garden, it was the community's response that had the most impact. Her yarden has major impact—it has gentle waves and paths that draw both the eye and feet into the space. Children from the neighborhood often come to be in her garden, to take fresh veggies back to their homes. Neighbors often stop by and ask questions. Many in her neighborhood have started to convert their own lawns into something else, on the basis of Linda's example. She's been featured in regional magazines, has given presentations and talks, and spreads the good word. Thus, we can see how a single effective lawn conversion doesn't just help us regenerate the land—it also starts regenerating and connecting our communities too.

Here on our homestead in western Pennsylvania, we moved in with about 1.5 acres of lawn. We converted about half of this into a range of beautiful gardens full of herbs, perennials for pollinators, berries, fruit trees, and annual vegetables. The other half we converted to a rotational grazing system with movable fences for our geese to graze. The geese mow the grass, lay eggs, and honk—nearly eliminating our need to use fossil fuel.

If you are planning on converting part of your lawn, I have a few suggestions to help you get started. The first and probably most important is to pay attention to your local regulations and ensure you are following them. I've seen too many people who disregard the laws of their township, homeowners' association, or some other body and then have their beautiful efforts destroyed. Work within the bounds of these associations, educating them as necessary, and remember that any kind of garden in a suburban area is highly visible. The second piece of advice I have, which comes from Linda, is to think of your garden not only as a garden but as a landscaping project. Work to make it beautiful, magical, and exciting for others to see—not an eyesore. This can help you avoid a lot of legal troubles with homeowners' associations and local laws. Some places and cultures in the world are more flexible, while others are not, so understanding your local context and constraints is very important. The third piece of advice is to start slow and convert small sections at a time—learn what it takes to maintain each and then convert more and more as you gain experience! Finally, find other examples in your community and talk with those people who are cultivating them, to get their advice.

The Land Steward

The land steward is a force of good in a broader ecosystem, providing healing and care to the land, especially to land that is not tended by anyone. Many people are not landowners but instead may be in an apartment, live in a van or tiny house, be renting, or otherwise. The land steward is an amazing role for you in this case, and it is so needed. You can "adopt" land, wild-tend, and scatter seeds wherever you go. This philosophy is a bit different than the others above—the above two assume you have access to some land or community land, and you are going to work fairly intensively.

The philosophy of the land steward is that you are serving the broader landscape, and that service might look different depending on where you are at the moment. Thus, a traveling land steward might join a river cleanup or help plant trees in one location and then, a few weeks later, spend some time scattering milkweed seeds across abandoned fields in another. Perhaps another day the land steward finds themselves teaching children about nature in a local forest and then volunteering to help in someone's garden. The land steward sees themselves as connected to their broader regional landscape and works hard to regenerate that landscape as they best can, wherever they may find themselves. Powerful tools for the land steward are community organizations who organize events, seed balls full of native seeds to scatter and replant, a deep knowledge of the ecosystem, and a caring heart.

Practice: Taking Up Regeneration as an Ovate

Which of the three models of regeneration above appeals to you? One of the ways you might find out is by visiting other places, seeing how people are regenerating the world around them, and discovering how you might take up this work. Consider these models—and possibly others—in the context of your own life. How might you tend, replant, or otherwise help heal the land? How can you begin or deepen your commitment to regenerating the land around you?

Story of the Present:

A TURNING POINT

When I was a child, in the summer and fall my family would go get ice cream. The ice cream shop happened to sit right in front of Sulphur Creek. The creek was full of foul-smelling, orange water from mines up in the mountains and had long been abandoned by the community. At eight years old, I had no idea of the history of the region or why this creek was so smelly and orange. I did know that upstream, the creek that joined this one—Otto Run—was healthy and that my family would often hike into the forest to visit Otto Run, playing in the shallow water and finding crayfish and salamanders. I was deeply saddened that only several miles downriver, my favorite creek flowed into one that was so poisoned.

It was definitely viewed as a bit odd for me to visit Sulphur Creek when we went to get ice cream. I would walk the 100 feet to where the creek flowed—a place that everyone else stayed away from because of the foulness and stench of the creek. But yet, I kept on visiting. I stood by Sulphur Creek and wrinkled my nose at the odor coming from the creek, seeing the bright, orange-stained rocks and the orange-yellow opaque water. I would always hear a quiet voice from the creek say, "Help me."

So many of the creeks I grew up around were just like Sulphur Creek. Communities literally turn their backs on these streams, creeks, and rivers; you'll notice there are never parks near them, no docks or steps built down into these creeks, houses are built without windows facing the creek, and no people are enjoying the water by fishing, tubing, or kayaking. In many places, waterways are places for people to gather and communities to connect. But when the waterway is poisoned, it scatters the community. The waterway is ignored like it is not there. It is not a place where anyone wants to spend time, and it is abandoned.

When I heard the voice from Sulphur Creek, I knew that I would not abandon this creek.

As I grew up, things began to change—not just for Sulphur Creek but all around the region. In 1995, the Sierra Club sued the US Environmental Protection Agency because the level of pollutants in many rivers throughout the region violated the Clean Water Act. The successful lawsuit required Pennsylvania to begin planning to clean up the worst of the rivers—at the top of this list was Sulphur Creek, which was discharging 99 percent more pollutants than allowable under the law. In 2007, a plan was put forth by the Pennsylvania Department of Conservation and supported by local communities who lived along the creek. I and many others were able to give public comments in favor of the plan. In the years after, a new acid mine drainage (AMD) remediation system, consisting of large ponds and passive aeration devices, was constructed to precipitate and help settle contaminants. And the slow healing process began.

As this was all going on, I continued to visit Sulphur Creek, offering blessings, healing, and friendship. For a long time, I was the only one who paid the creek any mind, but I knew this connection was important. As the years passed on, progress seemed infinitesimal—but each time, Sulphur Creek expressed more hope for the future.

At first, the change was imperceptible. Slightly less orange water, slightly less smell. But in a few years, the changes were obvious. In mid-2017, I visited Sulphur Creek and was overjoyed to realize that the smell had gone—the rocks were still stained bright orange, but the water was considerably less opaque and cloudy. The AMD remediation site had finally come into effect, and it was working!

Now as I write this in 2024, Sulphur Creek is on the path to recovery. The stains on the stones are slowly receding, and the fish are slowly returning. A community park has been expanded near the creek; debris and Japanese Knotweed that had obscured the creek at the park have been cleared away, and people can be seen walking along the water. In fact, the whole region has thousands of miles of rivers being cleaned up. Kayaking and tubing have become a new favorite hobby of locals in rivers that were once terribly polluted, and the brook trout are returning to the rivers—and the anglers are following. This physical regeneration is an important step, but not the only step, for healing our rivers and streams.

I continue to offer regular river-healing ceremonies and also volunteer to assist in river monitoring and cleanup. I recently asked the creek, "Do you want a new name? I feel like this name is the legacy of poison." Sulphur Creek's response was "Not yet."

Regeneration as a Bard

CULTURE AND HUMANITY

To return to our definition of regeneration, let's consider regeneration now in terms of ourselves and our communities. To regenerate means to take something that is damaged and help make it whole again, either by supporting its own natural healing processes (as in the case of herbal medicine helping heal the body) or through direct intervention. Every time I reread the story I've written above, tears come to my eyes. They come to my eyes because I have witnessed firsthand the way in which a polluted place that has been regenerated doesn't just support the living earth, but the human communities around those places. And that brings us to the work of regeneration as a Bard.

Prepandemic national statistics for the United States on human mental health and happiness were abysmal. They report that one in five Americans are clinically depressed, three in five Americans experience profound loneliness, 50 percent say they are unhappy, and the rate of adolescent mental health and suicide keeps climbing. The causes of these are numerous, but many studies point to the rise of digital media, increasingly toxic workplace cultures, disconnection from community, and how we spend our leisure time as some indications of what is going wrong. And things are going very, very wrong. These numbers—and many others like them—point to a painfully obvious truth: Our modern culture is destructive to its members and to the living earth, and only through deep and abiding change can we begin to find better ways of living with each other and the living earth. These numbers have grown much worse with the global pandemic and continual social upheaval into the 2020s. Regeneration means many things, but if we are going to work to regenerate our land and be a force for healing, we must root this work and ourselves in our human communities. If communities and people are cared for, they are more likely to care for the living earth.

Regenerating Our Local Cultures

Humans are inherently social animals. As we've explored in the chapters on Reconnection and Rewilding, I think it's important to recognize and honor our animal nature as part of our own nature; we want to be near others, to grow with them, to form bonds of friendship and love, and to feel a sense of belonging and purpose. As animals, we want to be free to express ourselves and feel like we are loved and welcomed. Modern culture does a great job of stripping all of this away from us, and the advent of social media and technologies has made it much worse. Thus, it is time to reclaim and regenerate our communities.

At an incredible natural-building school called Strawbale Studio in Lake Orion, Michigan, a community is gathering, growing, and spreading. Each month at the full moon, Deanne Bednar, the visionary of Strawbale Studio, offers a potluck for anyone who wants to visit. People come from all around the region for a chance to experience an alternative vision and to connect to a deeper sense of community. Sometimes at these events, we raise a roof or participate in a particularly difficult part of a natural build that requires many hands. Sometimes we sit by the fire, sharing stories, music, and songs. Sometimes we fire pizzas in the earth oven that was built by community hands from clay, sand, and straw. But that's not all that happens at these events: it offers opportunities for people to network, to share skills and tools, and to cultivate friendships.

What is happening at Strawbale Studio is starting to happen everywhere—people realizing that if we are going to have real communities, we can't wait for someone else to start them. We can build places where people are welcome to come, to grow together, to work together, and to find a different way forward. Creating these open, accessible, and welcoming community spaces is critical for the regeneration of human culture. The in-person connection is critical as part of these communities that heal.

Rather than thinking about these as a single community in a single place, think about them as planting seeds of a better human culture, seeds that take root, grow, and then expand outward. Seeds that are passed through the generations, with each new generation deepening these community-oriented and rehumanizing practices. These kinds of community spaces are seeds that can grow into mighty oaks, replacing the forests that were cut in our current age. If we plant enough of these seeds, we will regrow the forest and find ourselves in a new age, a better age, where people once again feel welcome, whole, valued, and connected to each other.

Part of this work is creating cultures where we are encouraged to be the best people we can be: nurturing, supportive, understanding, open minded, and willing to set disagreement aside. Many of these emerging cultures recognize that division, conflict, and disagreement are the foundations upon which modern media and social media are built, and thus work hard to offer a better approach through new models such as consensus-based decision-making, clear policies to support diverse voices and protect diverse people, and care-based interactions.

Consider for yourself: What kind of local culture already exists that you might want to join or strengthen? What kind of local culture doesn't exist that you could create? This can be as simple as inviting people over for potlucks around the fire, creating bardic jam sessions where people share music and stories, or community outings to hunt mushrooms. If the community doesn't exist, work to build it and they will come.

Regenerating Ourselves

While the statistics in mental health, loneliness, and the loss of connection already speak to the need for personal regenerative practices, the statistics on human physical health do not fare any better. Diseases of our modern age, such as diabetes, heart disease, and obesity, are widespread among human cultures. Now these same diseases are being spread among those other beings who have adapted to city living—and city eating—such as urban raccoons.[21] The evidence is overwhelming that modern life is destructive to the body, mind, and spirit. Thus, regenerative practices can be part of our work not only with our lands and cultures but also within ourselves.

Regeneration on a personal level can take many forms. A key practice in the regeneration of the body is looking to nature for healing. Nature is the ultimate healer—she can regenerate from a bare field to a mighty forest, given time. Just as she has the power to regenerate herself, she can regenerate each of us with her local and powerful medicines. Herbal-medicine practices combined with extended time in nature can profoundly regenerate the body in ways that pharmaceuticals and other practices from common culture cannot.

Herbal medicines work not only on the physical body but also on the spirit. A tree medicine such as Hawthorn (*Crataegus* spp.), for example, is a premier heart healer, strengthening and healing the physical heart and cardiovascular system, warding away heart disease, and facilitating more elasticity of the blood vessels. But Hawthorn's magic upon the emotional heart and human spirit is even more profound—she helps old wounds heal, creates a sheltered and protected space for overcoming trauma, and uplifts the spirits. Hawthorn is one of literally thousands of plants that grow globally that offer this kind of regenerative healing. As we explored in chapter 2, one of the best things we can do is learn how to reciprocate regenerative practices with plants just like Hawthorn: to seek our local healing plants and learn how to use them as medicine, and to collaborate with them to create regenerative spaces where they can live and thrive. This regeneration works both ways: as a way of regenerating our minds, bodies, and spirits, and as a way of regenerating the earth around us. While it is certainly beyond the scope of this work to offer guides to the many ways in which plant medicine and plant spirit medicine can be embraced, since this is an entire school of thought and life philosophy, the herbalism community offers many such resources through classes, conferences, community, and books.[22]

A second way in which nature heals is simply through spending time in nature, as we began to explore in chapters 1 and 3. Different practices are emerging around time in nature, particularly those that connect us with our ancient human roots. One such practice is earthing, which includes going barefoot or with minimal footwear, connecting to the soil. Another practice is forest bathing, where you simply spend quiet time relaxing in the forest (just like you would relax in a bath). Play, as we explore more in chapter 3, "Rewilding," can also be important here—mimicking wild animals, dancing in the sun, following trails or exploring new areas—allowing yourself to simply embrace your own wild nature and be an animal in a wild place. These practices aren't new; they are just new terms for people who are rediscovering the critical importance of spending time in nature for healing. One of my favorite practices in the summer is to strip down and run through the rain, barefoot and free (I call it my rain ritual, honoring the rains that nourish the earth). My favorite winter practice is to walk in the snow in random or creative patterns and create snow mandalas, just experiencing the joy of being out in the world that is so vibrant and alive.

Third, another major regenerative practice, is to cultivate a rich inner life—many of the practices in this book help do this. By cultivating a space in your life that can include valuable time in nature, various forms of meditation and spirit communication, tracking, adventures, and spirit-filled interactions, you create a space for nature to heal you. These practices are found throughout this book, but especially in chapter 6, "Reenchantment."

Since nature is the great healer, we can think about any time we spend in nature as regenerative on our bodies, our minds, and our spirits. Finding good friends to enjoy these nature-based experiences can be even more meaningful. Doing the work of regeneration as an Ovate builds our health, strength, and vitality and also allows us to spend time in the green.

Regeneration as a Druid

HEALING CEREMONIES, COSMOLOGY, AND MINDSETS

Sometimes we do not have the means to engage in deep regenerative work on a physical level. We may lack the ability, access to land, or resources to do this work. We see poisoned streams or logged forests; we see things happening on lands that we do not own or control and are unsure how we can possibly make a difference. While Ovate work is critically important to creating a brighter version of the present and beyond, we recognize that Ovate work is a particular kind of calling. The work that *every one of us can do*—including through our regenerated communities—is through ceremonies on behalf of the land. We've already explored the basics of ceremonies in chapters 1 and 3. I suggest that you build upon those basics when thinking about ceremonies that are focused on the regeneration and health of the land. Remember that ceremonies do not have to be stuffy or scripted but, rather, can be from the heart and involve movement, singing, dancing, and joy.

As we have already explored, ceremony is critical to the land to support vitality, healing, and growth. When you look across cultures old and new, one of the most consistent kinds of ceremonies in human cultures were those for the abundance and health of the land. Humans have done such ceremonies longer than recorded history. Nearly every human culture—save most modern Western ones—did such ceremonies. These ceremonies had several functions: They cleared away negative energies or ill forces that could cause harm, they provided energetic support for the health and growth of the land, and they established a clear role of caretaking on behalf of humans. Ceremonies on the land had lasting effects both physically and metaphysically and allowed the earth to be abundant, fertile, and rich, which benefits all.

Why do we see such ceremonies critical to a new shared vision for the future? Humans all over the world, including those in traditional and nonindustrial cultures and our human ancestors spanning millennia, recognize that ceremony is necessary for the well functioning of nature. Because these kinds of ceremonies have been done for so long, one could say that humans and nature evolved together through ceremony. When our lands no longer have access to ceremony performed on their behalf, all are missing a critical piece of what helps bring health, abundance, and vitality. These views on the role of ceremony on behalf of the land for the purposes of regeneration do not come out of one tradition but many—teachers and elders from many different traditions agree that ceremony is vital to a functional planet.

Further, when humans engage in ceremony, this work strengthens our own connections, realigns our hearts and spirits from the living earth, and puts us in a deeply reciprocal relationship with the land. These kinds of ceremonies help us shift our mindset toward one of care, of hope, and of recognizing the good that each of us has the power to do on this earth. That is, humans need these kinds of ceremonies as much as nature does.

The other piece here, of course, is that the very fabric of our landscape, in all parts of the globe, is so terribly strained and damaged. The damage of the last few centuries has been almost exclusively by human hands and is on a global scale. As any human survivor of violence understands, even after the body heals, the spirit may take a much-longer time to recover—and the damage to the spirit may linger long after the physical wounds have healed.

Thus, since humans have caused such deep wounds to our Mother Earth, we can create ceremonies to help her recover. Ceremonies of healing and regeneration literally heal the spirit of the land.

When we look across the world, many human cultures perform ceremonies on behalf of the land. One of my favorites is the wassailing ceremony, performed in the British Isles and later in North America. Wassailing ceremonies were an important part of the agricultural life because apples were a key crop: They provided a shelf-stable food, medicine, preservative (vinegar), and safe drink (fermented apple cider being safer than water in many places during earlier parts of human history). These wassailing ceremonies are once again being taken up all over Europe and North America in apple orchards, at homesteads, and at sacred retreat centers. In the same way, the Indigenous Micmac peoples engage in ceremonies for the abundance and health of maple trees, an important source of sugar. A successful apple crop or maple sap harvest not only supported the peoples who depended on the land but was a sign of a larger abundance, health, and vitality of the land that sustained them. Thus, as we move toward a more hopeful vision of the future, we recognize the need to bring ceremonies that benefit the health and vitality of the land to a more central place within our lives and within our communities.

The basic structure of the wassailing ceremony offers us insights on the nature of ceremonies for regeneration, health, and care. The community gathers in January around a strong, old apple tree in a larger apple orchard, one specifically selected to be the tree that receives the blessing on behalf of the orchard. Offerings of cider and toast were made, songs were sung, and the community would generate loud noises to scare away any malicious spirits or energy that may interfere with the apple harvest. The single tree receiving that blessing would radiate it out to the entire orchard, which was then energetically prepared to bring a physical harvest into the world. The timing was also important: The ceremony was (and still is) done on the old twelfth night, which translates to either January 6 or 17 in the modern calendars. January is the coldest and darkest month of the year and is also the time when apple trees are pruned and tended while dormant before they return to growth as the light of spring returns. Thus, the ceremony also recognized the importance of doing some energetic pruning work to make sure the orchard was abundant and full of life.

What would happen to this apple orchard without such a ceremony? Malicious entities, harmful negative-energy buildup, or other such maladies may energetically—and eventually physically—afflict the orchard. Problematic energies that are not addressed over time may slow the growth, may allow the trees to be more susceptible to disease, and may threaten the orchard. This view recognizes that it is not enough to physically *tend* the apple orchard in a holistic way, but rather, the orchard must be metaphysically tended as well. Apple trees have evolved with humans for thousands of years and have long been domesticated—they depend on human care. Now, imagine an entire landscape that has been without ceremonies for centuries. How damaged might that landscape become without the energetic support needed to grow and heal? How might the spirits of the land (chapter 2) feel about being abandoned?

In many places in the world, ceremonies like these may not have been done for many generations. Our lands are suffering energetically from the loss of such ceremonies—and we can see the physical ramifications of this loss: weakened ecosystems, pests and disease, groups of people who live upon the land who do not regard the land with a care mindset, and ultimately, loss of animal, plant, and insect life. Thus, by bringing regular ceremonies on behalf of the land back into our regular spiritual practice, we take up our ancestral role as caretakers, tenders, and healers of the land. Embracing this role can help reverse the course of the future both physically and energetically and provide blessing, light, and hope for the future.

Regeneration Ceremonies

The old Apple wassail ritual had a few key functions that are useful to explore here, since it provides us with a basic framework for all kinds of ceremonial work on behalf of the land:

- Offered blessing and protection (radiating out positive energy to counteract any negative energy)
- Focused on the strength, vitality, and health of the land
- Ritualized reciprocation and gratitude in the form of the offerings
- Performed by a community of people coming together
- Focused a ceremony in a small space and then radiated the blessing outward
- Repeated regularly in the same place
- Performed in a joyful and celebratory way

These six points are an excellent beginning to creating your own ceremonies on behalf of the land. And while we will offer some examples here, we stress that regeneration rituals on behalf of the land are best developed in localized contexts. That is, while I am giving you a road map of possibilities, a ceremony or set of ceremonies you develop for regenerative purposes on your land should be rooted in your immediate landscape with its specific needs, ecologies, and energies, as well as in the people who are performing the ceremony. I also want to assure you again that ceremonies do not have to be complex, with fancy clothing, elaborate scripts, and complicated symbols. In fact, in examining rituals that focused on the health, vitality, and protection of the land, they were often quite simple. It is your intent that matters the most. With guidance from spirit and one's own intuition, you can design a ceremony that is based on the needs of your land. What kinds of ceremonies might you create?

Druid practices for regeneration can focus on land healing, restoration, blessing, and strengthening—any aids that will directly help cleanse the land of negativity, alleviate suffering, and provide blessing to the land. When performing these ceremonies, however, it is important to recognize that the physical state of the land matters. If the land is abundant, growing, and producing, a ceremony that raises energy is appropriate and welcome.[23] But if the land is in a state of suffering from pollution, fires, habitat loss, or a myriad of other issues, you do not want to be raising energy. Think of this like a sick person—a sick person who is sleeping should be made to feel comfortable, not woken up with a jolt of energy. A person who is just a little worn out, however, might greatly benefit from a jolt of energy to get their spirits up again. Examining the specific situation on your landscape and carefully listening to the spirits of the land will help you understand and create the right kind of energetic support for the land.

River-Healing Ceremony

As the story of this chapter has unfolded, I have shared a three-century history of land extraction and damage that has taken place in western Pennsylvania, and this has been damaging to the waterways. I recognized that working with the local waterways was an excellent way to engage in ceremonies for regeneration, to engage in watershed healing. I have focused on waterways that were polluted and are now being treated and healed—a very different kind of ceremony would be used for streams that are actively undergoing damage and are still polluted.

For streams that were once polluted and are now healing, the ceremony is as follows. I go into my local watershed, and I collect water from clean sources: springs, snowfall, rivers, lakes. One local spring, Heffley Spring, is a very sacred place for me to collect healing waters, since it is also one visited by my ancestors. I ensure that these clean waters collected are in the same watershed that I will be healing. I combine these waters in a simple ceremony (calling in the four elements, asking for blessing) and create "healing waters" that I then energetically charge with drumming, placing the waters in the sun or full/new moon, and dancing and doing other ceremonial work as my intuition leads. I store these waters in a special shrine in my home, in a glass container. Then I carry these healing waters in a small vial with me to various damaged streams and sites. I ask permission of the waterway, and, if given permission, I release three drops of the healed waters into the waterway. If the location I am visiting is private and there are no other people around, I may do additional ceremony—drumming, flute playing, chanting, and raising energy for the waterway. If it is not private, I will sit quietly and offer a silent prayer. I regularly revisit these waterways with the healing waters to continue to offer blessing to the waters. Of course, all these streams feed into the Mississippi River basin. I am currently collaborating with some fellow Druids who live on other branches of the Mississippi River basin to do larger ceremonial work for the entire Mississippi.

For streams that are still full of acid mine drainage or other pollution and are suffering actively, I use a very different kind of ceremony, a palliative-care ceremony. In this case, I will come to the edge of the stream with an offering that can be placed in the river (such as fresh flowers, a pinch of offering herbs, a cup of spring water). I sit by the river and simply listen to the spirits of the river, hearing them, feeling the energies, and being present. I make my offering and may play light music or drum, holding space. I do not raise or direct energy unless specifically asked—in the case of this ceremony, the goal is to witness, hold space, and let the river know that I am present. The goal here is to hold space for the spirits of the land and let them know they are not alone. There is tremendous power in witnessing—when I look back at my experiences with Sulphur Creek as a child, I realize that I was engaged in a simple witnessing ceremony, not so different than what I've just described.

Cosmology: The Microcosm and Macrocosm

One of the reasons that ceremonies like the wassail and the river ceremony work is illustrated in the principle of the microcosm and the macrocosm. This philosophy, arising independently from Greece, ancient China, Mesopotamia, and Iran, as well as Indigenous cultures across the world, suggests that the human being (although small and singular) reflects the cosmos as a whole. More broadly, the principle suggests that smaller parts reflect the whole, and vice versa, and this interaction and reflection happen on every level of being, from the smallest atoms to the greatest galaxies. Thus, we see this principle in the wassailing ceremony: By honoring one tree, the blessing spreads to the whole orchard or even the whole region. If one offers a blessing in a small place and in a small way, that change can be reflected on the greater whole. We can also see the microcosm in the human being—the sacred geometry that unfolds in your own body (such as your hand: eight fingers, five digits on each hand, three bones per finger, two bones in your thumb, and one thumb) is the same mathematical equation—the Fibonacci sequence—that determines the spiral found throughout nature and even in the Milky Way galaxy.

What unfolds in the smallest of ways—the microcosm—also can be reflected as the whole. What happens locally impacts the whole, and vice versa. This principle is important in all aspects of regeneration and all of the 7 R's. In the case of a small place that you are wild-tending or creating a yarden, this energy can literally spread seeds and life outward. In the bardic arts within our own communities, an idea forms in one person and spreads outward like wildfire. In the Druid regeneration ceremonies, a focused blessing on one tree, waterway, or forest can offer blessing to the whole. In each case, we see that small actions of individual humans or small groups of humans can make a large impact. Modern Western culture teaches us to believe that we are insignificant, we cannot make a difference, and we cannot levy broader change. But this is one of many myths of modern culture, and thankfully, other, older philosophies offer us vision and hope. The principle of the microcosm/macrocosm suggests that you *can make a major difference* even by focusing your efforts in small ways. We explore the power of these concepts more in chapter 7, "ReVisioning."

Meditation and Reflection: Developing a Regenerative Mindset and Finding the Joy

When working on any level of regeneration, nurturing yourself and practicing methods for healing yourself is a critical step in these practices. Since the work of regeneration works with the principles of the microcosm and macrocosm—your inner life, your spirit, your emotions, and your psyche are all part of that microcosm. Sometimes, the most-important regenerative work we can do is within ourselves. Often, this work has to be done on ourselves before we can work to regenerate anything outside ourselves. We cannot be healers of this earth, of our communities, and of our world if we are broken inside. We cannot bring joy and light to a world that is dark if we ourselves are immersed in darkness.

The work of regeneration is hard work—for all three paths, it means often facing the results of poor behavior on the part of other humans—those who strip the land and harm the earth. It may mean working with people who feel broken or isolated. It may mean facing a lot of darkness, and a lot of despair, and being a beacon of light. To do this work fully and meaningfully, part of the work of regeneration is that vision of the future that is joyful, hopeful, and healed. How you find your inner joy, peace, and balance is different for each person. Mediation can help you tremendously by considering what feeds and nurtures you, what holds you back, and how you can seek regeneration and healing within. Consider the following meditation prompts as part of this work:

- What would you consider to be your most restful day in the last year? What did that day look like? How might you be able to re-create it more frequently?
- What are the things that bring you the most joy? How can you make sure those things come into your life most often?
- What wounds or trauma is still left unhealed within you? What is one step you can take now on the path to healing?
- How do you enact care in your life in small ways? How might you bring even more care into your community or to the earth?

Just like many other things, we can make the decision to live with a positive view, hope, and joy. When we go out into our land or into our community, we can radiate this hope, care, and joy into everything around us. But in order to have this joy, it is important for us to cultivate it!

A few simple practices can help you cultivate joy. First, each day consider writing down three joyful things that happened to you. Read the list often so you can see all the joy in your life. If you find yourself focusing on the bad in a situation, consider the flip side—what is good? Surround yourself with people who are uplifting and who also work to bring joy into their lives. Practice humor and invite in whimsy. Don't be afraid to experience and see the world through play. Spend time with children and play with them. Find the joy and embrace it with everything you have!

Story of the Future:

CLEAR CREEK

Several centuries have passed since the industrial boom in western Pennsylvania. While the past industry originally poisoned over 80 percent of the waterways and cut down 98 percent of the forests, it is but a distant memory. The people and the land have worked together, and much regeneration has taken place. Passive acid-mine-remediation systems, combined with reforestation and land regeneration, have healed the region. Forgotten springs have opened up, people are singing in the fields, and the forests stand tall overlooking the valleys below. The rivers and waterways are once again the lifeblood of this healed land. The River Otters have returned to the rivers, and with them Catfish, Rainbow Trout, Smallmouth Bass, Water Striders, and Salamanders. The Elk herds, reintroduced in the late twentieth century, now cover massive parts of the state, roaming free in the fields and forests. The people, too, roam wild and free, living from their land and honoring its bounty and majesty.

Through empathy, care, and consciously choosing to live in harmony with the land, directly dismissing the ways of their more-recent ancestors, they have found balance. They have not forgotten the legacy of industrialization or the damage that scarred the land before their time, but they have embraced a different path, a path of peace with the living earth. They have rebuilt their local communities again, embraced local foodways, and supported the rich and abundant land, strengthened by the bonds of a shared vision.

Dana's grandniece looks upon the creek once known as Sulphur Creek, with a broad smile. She has spearheaded an effort to rename the creek "Clear Creek" in honor of the creek's transformation, and the community has embraced this change, with a celebration and offerings to the creek. As the celebration winds down, she stands at the edge of the creek, listening to the spirit of the creek. The creek says, "Thank you. Come in and play." She laughs and, holding the hand of her daughter, goes down to the swimming hole to swim and search for crayfish.

DRUID
As above, so below, cleansings & blessings mindsets, mental fortitude, meditations
BARD
Cultivating community resilience, alternative economies, Creative Practices
Recovery
Adaptation
Opportunity
Flexibility
OVATE
Cultivating refugia, foraging & food security, ecological skills
Resilience

CHAPTER 5

Resilience

With Dana O'Driscoll

Story of the Past:

REFUGIA IN THE ICE AGE

The ice ages began nearly 2.4 million years ago. Ice ages are characterized by periods of extreme cold, when ice covers the earth and global temperatures plummet. Our last ice age started about 100,000 years ago, when ice covered much of the globe, including what is now nearly all of North America, northern Europe, and northern Asia. This made much of the land inhospitable to human beings along with a wide range of species not adapted to life on glaciers. Humans and many warmer-weather species in Europe moved to the land surrounding the Mediterranean Sea, where they survived sheltered from the largely inhospitable conditions in many other parts of the earth. All across the glaciers, small pockets of life, tucked away on a high point, a cliff, or a naturally warmer area, provided shelter, habitat, and a more hospitable microclimate.

On a small, protected valley in what will eventually be known as the Eastern United States, a beautiful river valley stands in stark contrast to the barren landscape that has been cleared by the movement of glaciers. Being protected on two sides by natural geological formations, this river valley is home to a wide variety of diverse trees, plants, and large and small mammals. Approximately twelve thousand years ago, the glaciers begin to recede, and warmth returned to the land. All the species that were hidden away in the refugia river valley began to spread out and began to repopulate the now-hospitable and warmer landscape. Like a seed sprouting forth, these plants, animals, insects, and others migrated farther and farther away, once again filling the land with abundant life where barren ice once stood.

INTRODUCING RESILIENCE

Resilience is a term I first learned as a permaculture practitioner—resilient ecosystems are those that can withstand hardship, recover quickly when faced with difficulty, and have the capacity to endure. In other words, a resilient ecosystem can withstand drought, flooding, fire, or other difficulties by being adaptable and flexible and having redundancies. Resilient plants are the often-maligned weeds, those weeds who take every opportunity to grow: who find a crack in the sidewalk, who immediately start to grow after disruption, or who outcompete less resilient plants. They are opportunistic (a.k.a. "invasive") species, taking advantage of new opportunities, finding niches, and gracefully adapting to change. Today, given the challenges before us, it is critical that we all learn the lessons of resilience and work to bring this into our lives, homes, and landscapes.

One of the most resilient and enduring plants in the world is the Japanese Knotweed (*Reynoutria japonica*). Japanese Knotweed is, as the name indicates, originally from Japan and survives in volcanic conditions; she is one of the first responder plants that helps the land heal after volcanic activity. Because of this, Japanese Knotweed is able to adapt to a wide variety of ecosystems and thrive in extreme conditions. She will continue to grow despite the best efforts of humans to remove her. Japanese Knotweed can withstand multiple direct applications of weed killer, and she can handle a wide variety of growing conditions (high and low soil pH, drought, high heat, extreme negative temperatures, flooding, chemical pollution, and more). Thus, Japanese Knotweed is probably one of the world's most resilient plants, able to resist almost anything that is thrown at her. I think it's interesting that Japanese Knotweed also is an outstanding source of food and medicine, as well as nectar for bees and insects. Japanese Knotweed is also one of the most hated and maligned plants for these very resilient features—modern-day humans don't like parts of nature that they cannot control and that spread wildly.

Another example of an incredibly resilient species is the Raccoon (*Procyon lotor*), an intelligent omnivorous mammal native to North America. Anyone who has lived in a region with Raccoons gets to know them quickly—they are extremely wily and able to break into all sorts of things (such as your shed full of chicken food or your chicken coop). Due to their opposable thumbs, dexterity, and fine motor control, they can unlock latches, solve puzzles, and break into all sorts of places. Raccoons are now quite effectively adapting to city life, with cities all over the world now having populations of Raccoons. A Raccoon is a being that embodies resiliency—a creature that is cunning, intelligent, persistent, and resourceful.

Japanese Knotweed and the Raccoon are wise spirit teachers that can offer us a number of lessons, perhaps the most powerful of those being *resilience*, lessons that I believe can help us ReVisioning our relationship to the world around us and that help us stay adaptable in challenging times. When we look to these two very powerful resilient beings in nature, they offer guidance about how to become resilient in an age of deep conflict and change. Even in a stable climate, all of nature—humans included—requires resourcefulness to survive, thrive, and adapt. But we are far from a stable time. And in the face of unprecedented challenges of the twenty-first century, resilience is a central concept that allows us to stay balanced, agile, and adaptable.

Resilience is the capacity to adapt, to endure, to quickly recover if damaged, and to successfully navigate changing conditions, and to do so joyfully and creatively. I would argue that it is probably the single most important concept that we can explore as humans living in the world today because we face a rapidly changing world with shifting challenges, a changing climate, and increasingly unstable social institutions. We cannot hold on to the stable past; we cannot bury our head in the sand. Instead, if we want to thrive in the current conditions, we must embrace an ever-changing and shifting future. Structures that are rigid fall and crumble, and we've seen a lot of that happening lately. The good news is that the human spirit is quite resilient. Just as our ancient human ancestors did before us, we can cultivate the resilience not only to survive but to thrive. To begin to explore the concept of resiliency in this chapter, let's look at these definitions, drawing on the help of Japanese Knotweed and Raccoon. The following five features encompass resiliency:

Recovery. Perhaps the most important defining feature of resilience is the ability to recover after a serious setback, challenge, or trauma. Rather than giving up, when you embrace recovery, you cultivate an ability to find a way forward. We see evidence of the recovery of nature everywhere—how quickly the opportunistic species grow after an area is cleared by humans or natural phenomena (such as the Japanese Knotweed); how quickly a forest that is burned or logged immediately starts to regrow; the ability of the tree to send up new shoots even if it was knocked down in a storm. Nature is literally full of examples of an innate ability to recover and move forward with explosive growth. The ability of nature to heal is one of nature's lessons that I always return to and that I am always in awe of—nature is the master of resiliency, and we can learn so much through observing her at work.

Adaptability. Adaptability is being able to pivot quickly in the event of trauma, adversity, or difficulty or simply if things are not working. Being adaptable allows us to face challenges and changes quickly and effectively. Raccoons are truly one of the most flexible, adaptable, and resilient of beings.

As they have been pushed out of their traditional habitats, raccoons have adapted to city life, living in attics, eating out of dumpsters, and continuing to cause mischief.

Accepting change. A necessary part of recovery and adaptability is being willing to accept change rather than hold on to the past, to ideas, practices, or beliefs that no longer serve us. It seems like a simple thing, but it is truly a difficult thing for humans to do, particularly in our less adaptable modern cultures. Again, we can look to nature for our guidance: Forest fires, floods, and tornadoes can cause irrevocable change. Rather than dwelling on what is lost, nature immediately springs to action and begins to heal. When the large trees are pulled down during a hurricane, nature is already prepared and immediately fills in that space, with new trees growing up to fill the canopy and the fungi kingdom coming to colonize and break down the tree.

Opportunistic. Capitalizing on opportunity is another key feature of resilience. Being opportunistic means being able to pivot quickly and take advantage of something that has changed. When I leave the door to our shed open, the raccoon will get into the bins of goose food stored there—taking up an opportunity. Opportunistic species of plants (what others may call "invasives") thrive on disturbances in the ecosystems—after a disturbance you will see Japanese Knotweed, Dandelion, and Burdock take root in otherwise hostile conditions.

Applying creativity. For human beings and mammals such as Raccoons, a lot of resiliency is about creative problem-solving. How can you do something in a new way? How can you meet a need when what you used to use to meet that need is no longer available? How can you approach something in a new way? How can you creatively apply your skills and resources to make a change? In permaculture design, my favorite of the design principles is "the problem is the solution," and I believe it epitomizes resiliency. In this principle, rather than seeing a problem as a problem, something to overcome or resist, you look at the problem to find the inherent solutions and opportunities that may be present in the problem. And then you tackle the problem from that angle, creatively and joyfully.

Now that we have a general sense of what resilience is all about, we now turn to our set of Ovate, Bard, and Druid practices to help us cultivate resilience in ourselves, our ecosystems, and our broader human communities.

Resilience as an Ovate

CULTIVATING REFUGIA, GROWING ECOLOGICAL SKILLS, AND FORAGING

As our story in the opening chapter shares, ice-age "refugia" were small pockets of life that survived and thrived despite difficult circumstances. On cliff walls, on a high point above the glaciers, in a sheltered valley between two mountains—these small pockets of life survived despite extremely inhospitable conditions. The concept of twenty-first-century refugia is not all that different. For example, in the United States, much of the land mass is cultivated: 40,000,000 acres of lawns, 70,000,000 acres of cities, nearly 400,000,000 million acres of crops, another 680,000,000 acres of pasture for domesticated animals—we can start to see a rather dismal picture when it comes to space for all other life.[24] Many of these human-dominated spaces are devoid of other life and actively seek to keep life from springing back up. Think of the chemical and mechanical ways in which life is suppressed (sprays, mowers, GMO crops, etc.). This essentially means that much of the current land use is extremely inhospitable to conditions for life.

Refugia are small pockets of life, small places for life to flourish and survive, despite the overwhelming challenges present in the broader landscape. They are places like my 5-acre homestead, which is surrounded by conventional farms and logged forests—the homestead is a refuge for life, and she and her partner actively work to rebuild the ecosystem to look like it used to before colonization, with an emphasis on supporting rare woodland medicinal species of plants and large insect and bird populations. Despite what is going on beyond that small pocket of life in conventional fields, life is thriving.

Thus, the principle of refugia is simple: Regenerate the ecosystem and invite life back in to survive and to thrive. And at some point in the future, your refugium can be the seed from which life can spring again, just like it did after the last ice age. I truly believe that cultivating refugia is a way to make a serious difference in the face of declines and mass extinctions—and can do a world of good. Your refugium may be the difference between a species surviving and thriving or going extinct—it can't get more impactful than that.

How can you cultivate refugia? Here are some basic principles:

- Learn about what species in your ecosystem are under threat and what ecosystems they need to thrive. This can be plants, insects, animals, fish, reptiles, or other invertebrates. While nearly all species are under threat at present, some can use some extra-special help. Select one or a few species to target on the basis of the space you have.

- Ensure that the refugium will be a safe space for as long as you can make it. This means making an agreement with anyone else who lives at your home not to disrupt the refugium, spray chemicals, mow, etc.
- Soil is the foundation of a healthy ecosystem. Work to build a healthy soil by using composting, sheet mulching, and other low-impact methods; again, avoid tilling or spraying.
- Consider what plants you might want to include (native plants) that can support the beings you want to support. Work to propagate these plants. For supporting insect populations, ensure that your plants have a range of bloom times. Often in the middle of the summer in temperate regions, there is a "nectar dearth"—to support insect populations, ensure you have blooming plants during all parts of your growing season.

Depending on where you live in the world, you may have a lot of support to do this work. In the US, states keep lists of rare and endangered species, and you can also visit websites such as the United Plant Savers (https://unitedplantsavers.org/). You can also visit the International Union for Conservation of Nature (IUCN) Red List website (https://www.iucnredlist.org/) for information on global species that are at risk. Also look up local or regional conservation organizations, since they may be able to help you choose plants, create habitat, and more. Once you've established your refugium, pay attention to how it grows and changes. Invite others in, talk about it, and spread the word of this good work.

Example Refugia: Wetland Refugium

At our homestead in western Pennsylvania, we've been working to cultivate three distinct refugia: a full-sun medicinal plant garden to support a range of at-risk and endangered plants, a forest ecosystem, and a wetland ecosystem down by our pond and stream. Our wetland refugium is a wonderful example of how you can consciously choose to cultivate refugia and support life. The wetland refugium includes a sunny spring-fed pond with a forested valley with many stones and mossy nooks and crannies. We worked to plant key threatened and at-risk species and create a healthy habitat. We do not allow fishing or any catching of species in our pond, we ask that people who visit respect the pond and the ecosystem, and we keep our own domestic waterfowl far away from the pond, to protect and preserve the ecosystem. We also have planted a range of Pennsylvania endangered or threatened wetland plants such as Spotted Joe Pye Weed (*Eutrochium maculatum*), Sweet Flag (*Acorus calamus*), and Highbush Cranberry (*Viburnum trilobum*). We developed our plant lists on the basis of examining the species lists released by our state's Department of Conservation of Natural Resources as well as through the United Plant Savers' Species at Risk List. We targeted supporting reptiles and amphibians, since they are at a higher risk than many other species at present in our state.

Our efforts have paid off, since we currently have a healthy population of Eastern Snapping Turtles (*Chelydra serpentina*), Eastern Red-Spotted Newt (*Notophthalmus viridescens*), Allegheny Mountain Dusky Salamander (*Desmognathus ochrophaeus*), American Bullfrog (*Lithobates catesbeianus*), Mountain Chorus Frog (*Pseudacris brachyphona*), and Northern Leopard frog (*Lithobates pipiens*), among other reptiles and amphibians. This refuge for all life is also a wonderful place to go connect with nature, engage in Sit Spot practices, and observe and interact.

Beyond the Baseline: Growing Ecological Knowledge and Skills for Resilience

In chapter 1, "Reconnection," we discussed the idea of Baseline Ecological Knowledge: the start of the journey of developing an intimate knowledge and relationship with the flora and fauna of your bioregion. This work is part of the ongoing work of reindigenizing to your local place—through knowledge, interaction, observation, and care you can build these kinship relationships with many other species. You might see it like getting to know your neighbors, and over time you develop friendships and relationships. However, how does one's Ecological Knowledge and relationship look like as they deepen over time? What happens with those relationships and those involved? And how does a deep relationship and deep Ecological Knowledge develop into resilience?

There is a well-known story that many students in the field of anthropology become acquainted with early on in their careers. The story involves an elderly Inuit woman who is interviewed by an anthropologist about her knowledge and skills, especially regarding surviving in the Arctic and subarctic climate, the traditional territory of Inuit people. The anthropologist is soon astonished to realize that the Inuit basically knows how to do everything that is essential for the people in the village to survive. She knows how to hunt seals, make clothes, make fire, gather medicine, read the weather, build a shelter, and preserve food, not to mention all the traditional cultural knowledge she had, such as songs and stories. As the conversation went on, the anthropologist became even more astounded as he realized that the woman was not unique or special; rather, their culture was designed to have *everyone have that kind of relationship to the land and nature.*

What that story teaches is that not only is Baseline Ecological Knowledge an important part of being human, it is also traditionally important that over time we all deepen those relationships and knowledge until we become intimately connected to the flora, fauna, landscape features, natural cycles, and more for where we live.

An example of how this might play out in our lives is to look at our relationship with our clothes. For example, it's highly likely that you had very little input into the making of the clothes you are wearing (the same holds true for me as well). We might choose what we wear and even where it comes from, and we can make more or less informed choices regarding the environmental impact and ethics of the clothes, including the kind of materials (recycled plastic? organic cotton, hemp, or bamboo?) and who produced it (fair trade or child labor?). However, it's pretty unlikely that you actually *made* the clothes you are wearing, and it is even more unlikely that you hand-harvested the material to make your clothes. And yet, isn't it astounding to think that not that long ago in human history, we all probably made our clothes by hand with materials we harvested ourselves? What happens if something changes and we can't get easy access to very cheap clothes made in mass quantities? How many people know how to make clothes by hand, let alone harvest materials to make clothes?

To take this a step further, did you know that humans have made clothes from animal hides and skins and fur for countless millennia? We've also made clothes out of all sorts of other materials, including Western Red Cedar bark, Stinging Nettle processed into wool, and Cattail fibers made into capes and hats. Figuring out how clothing was made traditionally in the bioregion you live in and what materials are still around to do so is a step toward deepening our ecological relationships and skills in an area. Actually, ethically hand-harvesting materials in a sacred manner and being able to make at least some clothes out of local materials are huge steps toward true resiliency—and will forever change your relationship to the mass quantities of clothes that are made and shipped around the globe every day. For example, one of the skills that I've learned in relationship to clothing is how to spin and create cordage from Dogbane, Milkweed, and Stinging nettle for a variety of purposes, including making jewelry. I also learned leatherworking to make shoes and bags.

Deep Ecological Knowledge allows you to go from simply observing nature to learning how to reciprocally meet at least some of your needs in nature—food, shelter, clothing, water, medicine, entertainment, and more.

Here are several other areas to explore around deepening your Ecological Knowledge in your bioregion:

- Develop a long-term, intimate connection with fire and wood. Learn to safely make fire in all conditions (wet, cold, dry, snow, etc.). Learn to cook on fire safely. Learn to sustainably harvest wood in your area in a way that *increases* forest health and helps *prevent* wildfire.

- Create your own medicinal herbal pharmacy both from wild-crafted and grown plants. Harvest them from your yard and bioregion in an ecologically regenerative way. Learn to make medicines from all of them to treat common, simple medical conditions such as cuts, scrapes, bumps, bruises, headaches, stress, insomnia, simple colds, and flus (all of these can be safely treated with simple herbal remedies!).

- Learn at least basic wilderness first aid and continue learning deeper levels of emergency medicine for you, your family, and your community.

- Learn to navigate your immediate area effortlessly without your smartphone, GPS, or even map and compass. Get to know the natural network of trails and paths through all the local nature areas. Grow your own mental map of the area.

- Study and learn the seasonal fluctuations and rhythms of all the flora and fauna of your area. What birds migrate in and out of your area and when? How and when do the pollinators emerge from winter and then disappear in the fall? What is the first wildflower and when does it appear? Which tree is the last to lose its leaves?

- Learn the common tracks and signs of the animal species in your area. Start big, with large mammals such as deer, elk, moose, coyote, wolf, bear, and cougar. But learn to recognize the small animals as well, such as voles, mice, shrews, and more. Don't restrict yourself to mammals. Learn to identify bird feathers and nests, amphibian egg masses and species, and even insect signs!

- Watch, observe, record, and pay deep attention to the major weather patterns of your area. What signs indicate a major shift in the weather? Where do the major storms come from? What indicates a major cold snap? A heat wave? How do you prepare?
- Learn to forage wild food, grow your own food, and enhance your and others' food security (see below).
- Learn how to build shelters from natural materials where you live. Camp frequently and learn to use less and less as you camp. Practice outdoor living in all weather conditions, including camping / building shelters in the rain, heat, snow/ winter, and other situations.
- Develop your own major passion and interest in any of the above or other related areas (fungi anyone?) and get really good at that area. Share your passion and talent with friends and community.

Wild-Food Foraging and Food Security

To zero in on one area of the list above, wild-food and wild-medicine foraging, is a great place to start to learn more. Foraging, or seeking out food and medicine in the local landscape, is one activity that can help you build a range of Ecological Knowledge, get you into nature, and help you deepen your practices of respectful interaction (see chapter 2), rewilding (chapter 3), and regeneration (chapter 4). Not all wild-food foraging practices are created equal, however, and one of the things I want to stress is that in order to build a *resilient* and *respectful* wild-food foraging practice, you need to consider not just what you take but what you give.

I started teaching wild-food foraging over ten years ago, after a lifetime of cultivating an ethical practice of foraging and working to regenerate damaged landscapes. I began teaching wild-food foraging with the naive and simple premise that if people understood that nature had value, they would honor and respect it, work to protect it, and cultivate a relationship with it. Unfortunately, this was not always the case. With increasing frequency, as new people get into wild-food foraging, I began to see something very different emerging: communities of people who see wild-food foraging as a treasure hunt, going into areas without any knowledge of the plant populations or sustainable harvesting techniques, and pillaging the ecosystem. I call this attitude the "Walmart of the forest," where one sees a forest just like a big-box store and goes in and takes whatever they want. And in these same communities, there is strong resistance to any discussion of limits, ethics of foraging, or cultivating reciprocation with the land. The term "pick shaming" is common in social media groups, and talking about limits, reciprocation, and good stewardship will get you kicked out of many groups (yes, I have gotten the boot more than once!). Unfortunately, in the wild-food community, we see the same colonizing and capitalist attitudes that pervade other aspects of Western society. In fact, I saw people whom I had taught years before engaged in these behaviors, for which, as their instructor, I was at least partially responsible.

Here in North America at least, one of the underlying issues is that nature is treated by most people in the twenty-first century no differently than it was treated in the sixteenth through nineteenth centuries: as a resource that you can take as much as you want from. The history of colonization in North America turned carefully cultivated and advanced agricultural systems (food forests) into food deserts and destroyed the way of life and culture of Indigenous peoples, who lived in harmony with nature. The current practices of land ownership and individualism stress this further—the assumption is that if it's your land, you can do what you want with it, regardless of how it impacts other life living there. As we explored in chapter 2, most of those are enculturated into this colonizing mindset when growing up and may not even be conscious of how much it impacts our assumptions and relationship with nature. This mindset drives a set of behaviors that are literally putting our planet—and all life—at risk. Thus, it increasingly becomes the case that at least some behavior surrounding wild-food foraging is a new take on a very old problem.

During the pandemic, I took a pause from teaching wild-food/medicine foraging to reflect on whether or not I was going to continue to teach it, given the "Walmart of the forest" mentality, and how I was going to shift my practices. I developed a set of ethical guidelines (offered below and shared on all my plant walks) as well as decided to teach only abundant or opportunistic (invasive) plants. By leveraging people's "pick all" mentality toward such things as Multiflora Rose (*Rosa multiflora*), Autumn Olive (*Elaeagnus umbellata*), and Garlic Mustard (*Alliaria petiolata*), I could take that existing energy and do some good in the ecosystem. I also began offering people seeds of plants that are commonly overharvested, such as Common Milkweed (*Asclepias syriaca*) and Ramps (*Allium tricoccum*), and encouraged them to cultivate their own wild patches and harvest those patches. I've been teaching this way for several years now, and the difference in what people who take my classes do with the knowledge is meaningful. I feel now that teaching foraging in this way is doing some good rather than causing more damage.

Thus, as you can see, there are a lot of layers to thinking about how we use anything from nature to provide for our own needs and do so in a way that establishes kinship relationships, reciprocation, and care for the broader ecosystem.

Given that, I offer the following three practices that can help you explore wild-food foraging from a resilient and ethical perspective—and I would suggest that these can be adapted to other practices where you are using nature directly for your own needs:

Harvest mindfully. Mindfully and ethically harvesting from the land to ensure sustainable harvesting and the long-term survival of wild food and medicines for the benefit of all life and future generations.

- Take only what you need. Harvest only what you need, and resist the urge to harvest everything. Find ways of preserving foods and wild medicine so that nothing goes to waste.
- Harvest in a way that sustains long-term populations. Be careful about how much you harvest, where you harvest, and when you harvest, to ensure that you are not damaging plant populations or harming individual plants. If you need to take a root harvest, it should be done only sustainably and when plants are in abundance. If you are taking a mushroom harvest, remember that mushrooms are the reproductive system; if you harvest them all, the mushroom can't reproduce. At the same time, recognize that some plants should be harvested as much as possible (opportunistic plant species should be harvested in abundance to control populations in the ecosystem).
- Harvest with gratitude and respect. Recognize the gift that nature is offering you, and harvest respectfully and with gratitude. Be thankful for the plant and the opportunity to harvest.

Tend the wilds. Our ancient human ancestors understood that creating a reciprocal relationship with nature was the only way to ensure a more bountiful harvest and sustain our lands so that they could sustain us in return. Thus, building in wild-tending practices and tending the wilds should be a counterpractice. See more about wild tending in chapter 3, "Rewilding," and chapter 4, "Regeneration." These practices can include the following:

- Observe plant population levels and scatter seeds of medicinal and edible plants that are native to ecosystems.
- Aggressively harvest opportunistic plant species to make room for diverse native species, and share this abundance with others.
- Choose wild lands where you closely monitor the ecosystem and tend the wilds.

Build your knowledge. Understand the plants that you are harvesting—how they grow, how they function ecologically, and the populations of plants in your area.

- Build your knowledge of ecology and plants. Recognize that there is a lot to know about plants, and that this is a lifetime of study. The more you know, the more you are able to apply to your foraging and wild-tending practice, as described in chapter 1 and expanded on above. Read books, attend workshops, and learn about how your plants function in the ecosystem: Where do they grow? How do they grow? What insects/animals depend on them? Which plants can you harvest as much as you want? Start by learning about a few plants and build from there.
- Observe and interact. Don't depend on the wisdom only in books, but get out into your local landscape, observe, and interact. Recognize that the populations in your local area of plants and mushrooms may be radically different than what you read about. Understand what is happening in the areas that you spend time in specifically, so you can be more mindful of your interaction.
- Connect, learn, and share with community. We can do more as a community than as individuals, so find ways to connect with like-minded others, building and sharing knowledge. The more we spread these principles and ethical-foraging approaches, the more good we can do in the world.

Story of the Present:

REFUGIA SPREAD

The last few centuries have been challenging on ecosystems globally. In the early part of the twenty-first century, ecosystems have degraded so much that almost a million species are at risk for extinction, with almost half of all biological life being destroyed in a few short decades. This is because humans continue to take up more and more of the planet's ecosystem, forcing life into smaller, segregated areas and then putting human pressure on those areas. As we move further into the twenty-first century, despair and sadness abound at what is happening. But humans respond, they change, and they adapt.

In one location in modern-day Ohio, a group of committed herbalists grow a nonprofit organization that creates a botanical sanctuary to preserve the most-delicate and most-endangered medicinal plant species. The herbalists work on producing lists of at-risk species, develop new forest-grown medicinal American Ginseng programs, and begin outreach. They train others about how to conserve medicinal plants and the ecosystems through which they belong, and they invite people to visit their sanctuary for classes, visits, and training. These herbalists don't stop at one plant sanctuary but instead create a larger network of botanical sanctuaries throughout North America.

And they aren't the only ones: As people begin to realize the power they have in cultivating change and protecting the ecosystem, a million refugia spring up in people's backyards and local parks. Humans begin to meet in small groups, organize, and act. They begin to set limits on their own consumption, build refugia, scatter seeds, harvest weeds, and start to believe in a better tomorrow. And as they individually turn toward these actions, they create broader shifts in their communities and world. These actions, great and small, begin to turn the tide, and more and more spaces are now green, growing, and healing.

Resilience as a Bard

RESKILLING, CULTURAL RESILIENCE, AND CREATIVE PRACTICES

As Wendell Berry notes in *The Unsettling of America: Culture and Agriculture*,[25] one of the things our civilization has demanded is increasing degrees of specialization—and with the rise of super-specialists, we lose our ability to take care of our basic human needs. He advocates a return to the ways of the generalist, where we cultivate a wide range of skills—and, in so doing—develop more-powerful methods of being resilient. If you think about it, it makes a ton of sense; as we have already been exploring, throughout human prehistory and history, nearly all humans had a basic set of skills that allowed them to clothe themselves, feed themselves, provide shelter, find clean water, perform basic healing, and take care of a host of other basic needs. It is only with the rise of industrialization and the modern era that these have been forgotten. But if we are going to be more resilient, it's useful to think about how we can return to some of these ancestral ways. Additionally, just as our ancestors knew and understood, resilience is both an individual and a community practice, and it requires all the connection and creativity that we can muster.

Physical Resilience: Reskilling

Resilience in our lives means being better prepared for things that may occur that are unprecedented, which is now the norm rather than the exception. If the recent global pandemic, growing extreme-weather events, and other social upheavals have taught us anything, it is that the systems upon which we build our lives are not going to continue to be stable, and it's up to us to build skill sets that allow us to provide some of our own needs.

When we think about our needs, Maslow's hierarchy of needs is a good place to start. We all need food, clothing, clean water, shelter, and, in colder climates, heat. At present, most humans have long depended on others (corporations, larger consumer systems, etc.) to provide those basic needs.

Reskilling is the practice of learning a variety of skills that can help you take care of your own needs and the needs of those around you. The reason that it is called "re" skilling is that we are relearning skills that our ancestors had. Thus, reskilling is the practice of building a knowledge base of skills that will help you be more resilient regardless of what happens locally, regionally, nationally, or globally.

In previous times, as our story of the Inuit woman above explored, nearly everyone had a set of baseline skills focusing on meeting their everyday human needs: Everyone knew how to keep themselves safe, warm, and fed. Thus, a list of basic skills includes growing or foraging (or both) some of your own food (see above), learning food preservation techniques (canning, dehydrating, fermenting, brewing), learning how to start and maintain a fire, building simple shelters, learning about water purification, and learning how to mend clothing, among others. But within communities, people would also specialize—the village healer, the village blacksmith, the weaver, the cobbler, a specialist in animal husbandry and animal medicine, the brewer, and so on. A useful approach to reskilling is to think about this not only individually but in terms of your broader community.

To begin to think about reskilling, you might consider the following questions:

- What skills are you most excited to learn? Follow the flow of your interests and enthusiasm.
- What can you learn locally or from people you know? While online sources and books are great ways of learning, there are few substitutions to learning from someone in person and practicing together.
- What skills do you see as most necessary to you, your family, and your community at present? What skills do you think are missing?
- What skills may best fit into your current life with your current limitations and opportunities? It is better to practice a skill that you can do well, given your own limitations, such as limitations with space, resources, etc.

The above list can help you get started. This second list offers just a small list of skills you might consider exploring:

- Nourishment: gardening, forest gardening, wild-food foraging, food preservation (brewing, fermenting, drying, canning, freezing), seed saving, animal husbandry, solar cooking, earth ovens, open-fire cooking, other conventional cooking alternatives
- Clothing: mending, spinning, weaving, natural dyes, learning how to work with animal fibers, growing natural fibers (flax, hemp, cotton, linen)

- Shelter and warmth: basic wilderness survival, fire starting, fire tending, wood chopping, woodlot management, building basic shelters, carpentry, natural building and cob, rocket stoves and other low-energy options
- Crafts: woodworking, woodcarving, blacksmithing, bookbinding, cobbling, leatherworking, tanning hides, pottery, basket weaving

As you can see, nobody can accomplish all of these skills—the set of all the above is accomplished in a community. We suggest picking one or more and starting to learn—preferably with friends or family.

Finally, with our emphasis on reskilling as resiliency, we also want to caution against the "prepper" mentality. In a common vein of modern society, we have the preppers, who typically amass boatloads of stuff that will keep them insulated against whatever may come. And while it is always a good idea to have a small stockpile of supplies for short-term issues, we recognize that it is skills—not stuff—that will help us transition to resilient, earth-honoring societies. Why is this so? Because you will run out of this stuff, and stuff can be stolen or damaged. Skills are with you anywhere you go, and skills can be shared freely with others. Thus, we suggest you invest your time and money into learning skills and building relationships with your neighbors over the prepper mentality of hoarding supplies.

Cultivating Community Resilience

Part of cultivating physical resilience is thinking about how to transition at least some of our basic needs to a community and individual level rather than assuming that corporations and governments will provide them. Thus, our next question is this: What do resilient human cultures look like? These are cultures that have resilience in relationship to place, cultures that have adaptability and redundancy and are able to provide for the needs of the people and lands. These are cultures with regional and localized systems of food and goods production that are able to meet the needs of those who live within these cultures, strong community bonds, and the ability to come together and overcome challenges. And, as my example shows, they are also cultures that care for and live in balance with their local ecosystems, tending them and ensuring abundance for all life and future generations.

While writing this chapter, I had a chance to visit the island nation of St. Vincent and the Grenadines in the Caribbean. It struck me how resilient this culture is: strong community bonds with an incredible friendliness (everyone says hello), local food systems that were providing the bulk of what was eaten, food systems that were integrated into every home and community, food systems entirely grown by farmers who used hand-powered and human-powered methods of production, systems of distribution of food that were localized (e.g., you put what you have available out for others to see, and they trade or purchase), and employment of local building materials and methods. But more than that, one of the most striking things about this experience was the deep love, reverence, and respect that people showed their land. And the deep respect that they showed me as a visitor. I was able to meet with five different farmers growing a range of food and medicine, and I was just stunned not only by their wide-ranging and deep knowledge of the food, medicine, and other resources of the landscape, but also by their care of the land. These farmers loved their land; they farmed without fossil fuels, without external inputs, and in ways that were respectful of their land. Their farms were often a thirty-to-forty-five-minute hike into the mountains, where they carried up everything they needed and carried their produce back down by hand. It was an honor to witness. While I had observed this web of interconnections on a small scale at individual places or eco-villages, such as Dancing Rabbit Ecovillage in Missouri, USA, I had never witnessed it on a culture-wide scale. I found it particularly interesting to see the relationship between these localized, resilient cultures and their deep love and care for the land.

Humans have always been tribal and social, as are many of our animal kin. Thus, rather than thinking about resilience as an individual problem, you might think about it as a community or group effort. What can you do now to support a more resilient community? How can you help other members of your community become resilient and support strong bonds between people? Supporting a local food system, community garden, or farmers' market is a very clear choice—even if you aren't able to grow your own food, network, and provide resources to those that are; the stronger a local and regional food system is, the more resilient your community is. This is also where other community groups such as permaculture meet-ups (who share tools, resources, and knowledge), reskilling communities (who work to build traditional skills among members), and earth skills gatherings can come in. Organizations and events that bring people together to build bonds of friendship also matter here. The point is that you can cultivate a lot of resilience in your life by joining with others.

A great way to focus on community resilience is to create community skill shares and reskilling fairs. You can do this on any scale, ranging from inviting a few friends over, each to teach what they know, to creating a larger community or region-wide event. These skill shares can focus on a particular set of skills (e.g., traditional cooking methods, fire-cooking methods, woodworking), or they can be open to any human skill, craft, and art form.

Taking Up a Bardic Creative Practice as Resilience

Another great way of cultivating personal resilience is to find ways of managing difficult emotions, fear, and anxiety surrounding the current state of the world. Many people find that taking up a creative, bardic practice can both reskill and also give you a creative outlet from which to find grounding and stability. In fact, in my 2018 Mount Hameus research through the Order of Bards, Ovates, and Druids[26] on the bardic arts, my surveys and interviews with over two hundred bardic practitioners showed just how powerful the bardic arts were in helping people manage emotions, anxiety, grief, and so much more. Creative practices were a lifeline for people to process pain and trauma, find balance, and emerge whole. Thus, a bardic art gives you both a chance to practice a new skill and the added benefit of emotional resilience.

However, another problem of modern culture is that it pushes us to consume others' mass-produced creative works and disempowers us from creating our own. Creativity, and connecting with what we Druids call "Awen" or divine/flowing inspiration, allows us to get deeply in tune with our own thoughts, spirits, and subconscious. Every human is born with creativity and the ability to learn a set of creative skills. We can learn this from seeing small children—they are never afraid to create and to play.

My suggestion is to find a creative practice that you are excited to learn, give yourself time and space without expectations to learn it, and see what happens. There are many options: literary, performative, craft, or artistic. It is only when we have been discouraged repeatedly that we lose that creative spirit or begin to say, "I'm not creative; I'm not talented." In fact—you are! If you see this practice not as something to perfect or commercialize, but as a part of your own spiritual journey, that can be very helpful. If you embrace the process of creating the work as a sacred and joyful experience rather than a product, that is even more helpful to breaking out of the cultural norms and expectations and allowing the Awen to flow. Creating is a wonderful way of healing and exploring our deepest spirits. By reframing your creative practice as a spiritual practice, the goal becomes not to produce some good or flawless creation but, rather, simply to enjoy the act of creation itself.

Listening, watching, and observing the land itself while sitting quietly can be a profound exercise in creativity and can help cultivate a range of the 7 R's. What song is the land singing to you? Or what song does the land want to hear? What is calling out to be painted or drawn from nature? What story is wanting to be told or heard from the trees, the creek, the ocean, the mountain, or even just the diversity of plants in our front yard? What poem might arise from the elegant blooming of a daisy in a meadow or from the myriad colors of the sun setting over a lake? We explore cocreating visions with nature more in chapter 7, "ReVisioning."

Further, when we start learning the bardic arts, and as we engage in more-challenging work as a Bard, we are regularly confronted with difficult situations where we can cultivate resilience: creativity, adaptability, and taking new opportunities. These practices require us to confront our own fears and our own struggles and, occasionally, to deal with failures. If we can take what we've learned from these practices and connect them to other aspects of our lives, it will cultivate a general resilience that can be helpful.

Financial Resilience and Alternative Economics

A final consideration here is considering resilience in terms of your own capital. Capital is most often considered financial, and yet, throughout history, humans used alternative means such as gift economies or barter systems. The truth is, most of us have never experienced alternative economic systems to those dominant in our cultures, and yet, these are well worth exploring. Drawing upon the principles of financial permaculture, you might consider how to cultivate financial resilience through any of the following:

- Reducing expenses and finding ways of repurposing, restoring, and otherwise getting things for free (waste is a resource!)
- Exploring trading and barter systems, where goods or services are exchanged directly without the need for cash
- Developing multiple income streams so that if a major income stream dries up, you still have others (especially exploring passive or low-investment income streams)
- Exploring eight forms of capital and their currency: social, material, financial, living, intellectual, experiential, spiritual, and cultural,[27] and considering the many different kinds of capital you already have or can cultivate
- Reorienting your relationship both with money and time can take many forms: meditative, practical, or social. A very useful approach for this is recognizing how much time your current job takes and how that translates to your real working wage (ideas for this can be found in *Your Money or Your Life* by Vicki Robin and Joe Dominguez).[28]

- Building gift economies, where reciprocity and relationship are at the center of the "gifting" of goods and services. If everyone is gifting to others, all needs can be met.

A Resilient System in Action: The Outdoor Kitchen

You can combine many of the categories above to cultivate resilience in one or more areas of your life. One of the areas that I've been focusing on for a long time is connected to natural building, bardic arts, foraging, growing food, and cooking. We began our outdoor kitchen project some years ago, which currently houses a sitting area, earth oven, and maple sap boiler/grill, with plans to expand in the future. The earth oven site was chosen and cleared in a reverent way, during which we moved many of the plants to other parts of the property. The oven itself was almost entirely constructed from the land, using clay, sand, straw, and stones as well as recycled wine and beer bottles from friends. We decorated the oven with a mosaic of broken mugs and plates saved over the years. And now we've been learning the fine art of bread baking and baking all sorts of other foods in the earth oven—such as our garden vegetables, stews, quiches from eggs from our birds, and much more. And we gather sap from the trees and boil it down, inviting others in our family and community to participate in the fun.

There are so many things that this outdoor kitchen project touches on in the above list: We are no longer dependent on electricity or fossil fuels for cooking our food, we have a way to cook year-round if something were to happen to the electricity grid, we built this oven with the free help of friends (whom we now feed with the oven—gift economy in action), we can grow food right from the land or use wild foods we forage, and we can fire the oven by using only sticks and branches that naturally fall from the trees on our property. The entire practice is community based, with many opportunities to invite others to fire up the oven and tend it, bake pizzas and breads, and simply enjoy each other's company. One three-hour firing of the oven gives us enough baking time to bake more than twenty pizzas, breads, casseroles, vegetables, and more, making it one of the most efficient uses of fuel. Most importantly, this is slow and connected food, delicious, sacred, and nourishing. I share the outdoor kitchen project as an example of a resilient system in action—consider your own life and design one or more projects like this, one that allows you to stack many different functions to help cultivate resiliency.

Resilience as a Druid

COSMOLOGY AND CULTIVATING SPIRITUAL RESILIENCE

The age that we live in presents unprecedented challenges and difficulties that are only going to increase throughout our lifetimes and the lives of our descendants. One of the reasons that people have spiritual paths is that it helps us get through difficult situations. And right now, spiritually cultivating resilience is a core practice—building the mental, spiritual, and physical fortitude begins with us. The great news is that nature is the ultimate guide for us to learn resiliency—we can look to our allies such as Japanese Knotweed and Raccoon, and so many others, for incredible examples of the resilient, healing power of the living earth. We, too, are part of nature and are capable of cultivating an adaptable, resilient spirit.

So, this brings me to the next question: What do resilient humans look like? What spiritual practices do they have? I would argue that these are people who are emotionally expressive and connective, spiritually aware, and sensitive but also strong, focused, and skilled enough to get things done. And before we begin this section, let me just say this—what I'm writing here is hard stuff. It is hard because we have entire lifetimes of indoctrination designed to keep us helpless, fearful, and dependent on the system. And yet, it is critical internal personal and spiritual work necessary for us to build a better tomorrow. So, let's take another step on that journey.

Cosmology: As Above, So Below, As Within, So Without: The Physical/ Metaphysical Nature of the World

An ancient and well-known magical philosophy, written by Hermes Trismegistus from the ancient Hellenistic era, sums up these relationships and has been adapted to the modern age with the phrase "As above, so below, as within, so without." This adage expresses the relationships between the world of spirit and the world of matter, both external to us or within us. We recognize that the world as we know it is made up of things both observable and nonobservable, and through our own senses and intuition, we can explore all of these things, learn, and grow from them. One of the things that this book explores is the relationship between the physical world (also described as the "material world" or the "material plane") and everything else. By everything else, I mean several things. First is the world of spirit. Just as humans have a soul or spirit that transcends our physical bodies, so does everything in the world have a spirit that transcends matter (we explored this concept first in chapter 2 in our discussion of animism). The world of spirit overlies the world of matter and can intersect this world. Thus, the first part of this adage explores why ceremony works, and why attending to things on the metaphysical can be as effective as on the physical.

Part of the "As within, so without" adage also refers to the incredible power we have within us: our intuition, our subconscious, our souls—while these things are not tangible, they are no less real. What the adage suggests is that when we cultivate changes within ourselves—such as the practice of cultivating inner resiliency we describe in this section—these changes will manifest into the world around us. This philosophy also suggests that the more that we are able to get in touch with those deepest parts of ourselves, the more we can become, in the framework of Carl Jung,[29] a whole, healed, and "individuated" being who is capable of great things in the world.

As we've explored in earlier chapters, this principle also rests on ideas of the microcosm and the macrocosm (chapter 4). Although we may be one person, we, as a microcosm, can bring about great changes in that broader macrocosm. And as we will explore chapter 7, these two principles working hand and hand can give us a more beautiful vision and reality of a healed world. Thus, in this section we explore a range of "inner" practices that can ultimately help us with the work outlined not only with Resilience, but in all 7 R's.

Cleansing and Blessing Ceremonies

One spiritual tool that is particularly useful for cultivating resilience is spiritual cleansing and blessing practices. Because humans have almost a natural instinct to focus on the negative aspects of situations, to continue to live through past trauma, and to bring that energy into our lives, cleansing and blessing practices help us move past our trauma, grief, and sadness and be whole, healed, and resilient. In other words, doing these kinds of practices regularly helps us have an upright, sound perspective. Ceremonial practices of cleansing and blessing can help us energetically cleanse any energy, attitudes, beliefs, trauma, or other things no longer serving us, and then set up the right energetic conditions for moving forward in a positive manner.

Smoke cleansing, healing, and blessing practices exist in many different cultures worldwide, where plant matter (resin, leaves, flowers, or wood) is burned in a bundle or on a live coal and used to clear a space or person. For example, the Scottish practice of saining involves burning large amounts of juniper in a cauldron or bonfire to release a good deal of smoke; this is combined with a water blessing and can be used to clear houses, livestock, or people. The Vedas, ancient Hindu texts written in Sanskrit, are one of the oldest written records of smoke cleansing. This approach used various botanicals, such as sandalwood and turmeric, in the form of incense to help heal and bless a space for the healing of the human body and spirit. In the traditions of Buddhism, Shinto, and Taoism, smoke is burned not only in the veneration of the ancestors in temples, while in traditional Chinese medicine, smoke was burned for health and wellness. In Africa, both spiritual leaders and healers burned herbs on charcoal or through fire to smoke, which is moved around a person for various purposes, including to heal or connect with the world of spirits. Tying to the ancient Hindu, African, and Chinese uses of healing smoke, scientific research on the use of medicinal smoke by researchers[30] examined fifty different smoke blends and found that 256 plant species were used. They found that smoke had beneficial impacts on the skin, the brain, the heart, and the pulmonary system, as well as purifying the air, keeping harmful insects at bay. Smoke may be inhaled, burned, or blown on particular parts of the body in these various countries' traditions, including Mugwort, Agarwood, and Sandalwood. When we look at these varying and global traditions, we can see that many cultures developed a relationship with smoke as an aid for clearing, blessing, and good health.

A simple smoke-clearing ceremony begins with using botanicals—herbs, resins, leaves, sticks, and flowers—gathered locally, dried, and then either bundled into a stick or ground and burned on active charcoal. In line with this book and the rewilding and localizing practices we offer, I strongly suggest learning some of the herbs that can be burned in your local ecosystem. Using practices of reverence (outlined in chapter 2), you can seek herbs in your local system, in your garden, or even from your kitchen. These herbs might include many from a typical herb garden: Mugwort, Oregano, Sage, Rosemary, and Lavender are good choices. Another great choice is using conifers that have burnable needles and resins, such as those in the Pine, Spruce, or Rir families, or those with aromatic woods, such as Sassafras. You can also visit your spice rack to use Cinnamon, Sage, Nutmeg, Star Anise, Bay Leaf, or Clove. The best part about developing your own local blend is the experimentation—start identifying plants, smelling them, burning them, and seeing what happens. You can use a single herb or combine it into blends. Also remember, in line with regenerative philosophies, while many metaphysical shops will sell traditional woods, spices, resins, and herbs such as Sandalwood, White Sage, Agarwood, Frankincense, and Copal, nearly all of these plants are endangered or threatened due to human overharvesting.

Smoke-clearing ceremony. A simple smoke-clearing ceremony can be done with great effect. First, take three deep breaths to bring yourself into full presence in the moment. Sit with the herbs, feeling their energy and presence. Light your herbs, offering your gratitude and thanks. You can say something like, "Spirits of these plants and trees, I offer you my gratitude.

You who have worked with humans for countless millennia, please offer me your cleansing and blessing." Then light the herbs. Ensure they are burning well by offering them your breath. Then bring the smoke around you, from head to toe. Envision the smoke clearing you of negativity, outside influences, pain, and anything else you no longer want to carry. See the energy of the herbs settling into your skin to form a protective energetic layer. After this, you could smoke-cleanse another person (human or nonhuman) or your home or use this to help establish sacred space. This ceremony can be adopted in a variety of different ways for your own needs.

Stepping back from this ceremony, what this offers is a powerful way to connect both with our ancient ancestral roots and the plant kingdom to provide us with energetic ways of clearing and supporting ourselves for the work ahead. If we build smoke-cleansing, blessing, and protection practices into our daily lives, we are taking a powerful step toward being the resilient beings that we are capable of being.

Building Mental and Spiritual Fortitude

When you study any kind of wilderness survival, one of the most important things you learn is to keep a *positive mental attitude* toward a difficult situation. That is, half the battle is staying positive and flexible and having a good mindset along with the many skills above: adaptability, recovery, accepting change, and being opportunistic. This is not a skill set that many people are brought up to have. In Western consumer culture, we are purposefully taught to be passive recipients of culture and to buy our way out of problems, to allow others to take care of our needs. In other words, if you live in any modern consumer culture, you have been socialized into a set of behaviors that are actually taking you in the *opposite direction* of resilience. Part of this is getting out of our own minds and out of our screens to learn how to nourish ourselves through these resilient actions.

Resiliency is a combination of having the right mindset and being able to solve problems (drawing upon skills, knowledge, and resources). It is about having a positive mindset and cultivating a creative and adaptable way of thinking, along with having a toolbox of skills, techniques, and knowledge that you can draw upon as needed. Ultimately, resilience is a mindset that we carry with us. We cannot control the world around us, and we certainly cannot stop the large-scale impacts of anthropomorphic climate change and how they are impacting our present and future. But we have full control over how we learn to adapt, respond, and move through this present. Resilience is part of what helps us create a more hopeful and joyous future. Being resilient helps us cultivate hope, because we know, inside ourselves, that we can approach the present and future with confidence and not fear. So, let's explore some methods for building mental and spiritual fortitude.

Cultivating Growth Mindsets

It's very helpful to take an inventory of which resilient skills you already have and which you might want to cultivate. Knowing yourself and having a metacognitive sense of who you are (e.g., knowing your strengths, why you respond in certain ways) can help you cultivate resilience. For example, one important skill for resilience is how you handle difficulty or failure. Do you give up? Shut down? Berate yourself? Or do you rise to the occasion, trying something new and taking the difficulty as an opportunity to learn and try again? This is a matter of mindset. Psychologist Carol Dweck[31] identified two primary mindsets that people have that greatly impact their ability to be resilient: growth and fixed. Individuals with a growth mindset recognize that struggle, difficulty, and failure are part of one's ability to learn, and see these as growth opportunities. Individuals with fixed mindsets believe that intelligence and skills are "fixed," and thus see failure, struggle, or difficulty as poor reflections on themselves, so they avoid struggle or shut down in the face of difficulty. Growth mindsets are, therefore, tied to a host of resilient qualities: flexibility, adaptation, recovery from failure, and keeping a positive attitude despite the difficulty. One of the most comprehensive parts of the larger body of research on mindsets is the long-term learning outcomes for individuals with growth and fixed mindsets. People with growth mindsets are more resilient but also learn more, grow more, and perform better in the long term. The difficulty in mindsets is that modern culture, lifestyles, and education systems often cultivate fixed mindsets in people—so many of us have some work to do.

How might you cultivate a growth mindset? You can use meditation and self-reflection to explore your own mindset and work to change it. Consider this approach: Start by meditating on the last three major struggles or failures that you have experienced. How did you respond? From the perspective of mindset, what could you have done differently? In your inner vision, play out an alternative—you responding in the best way possible. Hold that firmly in your mind. What does that feel like? Take that feeling with you. The next time you are in a situation that is challenging or difficult or requires your resiliency, return to that feeling and take a moment for a few deep breaths. Return to that meditation, then work to shift your mindset. This visualization is a powerful magical act that allows you to resee the past and build a resilient set of skills for the future.

Spheres-of-Influence Meditation

Another part of becoming resilient is recognizing the difference between perceived adversity versus actual adversity. If modern media, news, social media, politics, and corporations do one thing well, it is making faraway problems seem like they are immediate, personal problems for all of us. Sociologist Barry Glassner[32] writes about the "culture of fear" that pervades the United States, which also has spread to many other countries globally. Glassner argues that news media and, now, social media perpetuate a culture of fear tied to things that aren't actually important, while undermining real and present dangers. Fear makes us less resilient and more likely to give up our personal power, our freedoms, and our ability to reason and think for ourselves. This is biological—when we are in fight-or-flight mode, our sympathetic nervous systems take over, causing physiological changes to our brains and bodies and keeping us in a state of readiness. Long-term responses in our sympathetic nervous systems create adrenal fatigue and exhaustion, which has its own set of very serious mental and physical health challenges. By regaining control of this through examining our spheres of influence and other meditation and spiritual work, we can build more resilience.

Considering our own spheres of influence can help us recognize what things we should legitimately be concerned about and take productive action to address and solve versus which things are simply fear inducing to control us.

For this, draw a circle on the paper and put you in the center of the circle. Now draw a set of concentric circles outward and label them "direct control," "large influence," "small influence," and "out of my control." Now consider everything that is around you—what are the things you have direct control over? This might be your daily life—your decisions, what you eat, what you wear, where you go, how you choose to make money, and so on. Now consider the things that you have a large influence over, things such as the community garden where you volunteer, your employees under you at work, and so on. Where might you have some small influence? In political elections, local or regional politics, and other places in your community. And what, essentially, is out of your control? Now meditate on this sphere of influence with regard to the things that bring you stress, anxiety, and fear. How much of it is within your immediate sphere? How much of it is outside that sphere?

In doing this meditation, see how much of your focus can be shifted to the first three areas in the sphere—the areas that you have at least some control over. It is easy to be afraid and reactive to things outside our control—that's how the system is designed to operate to keep you feeling rather than thinking or doing. By focusing instead on what is directly in your control, you can begin to think about *actions* rather than *reactions*.

Beyond this exercise, it is useful to keep in mind your spheres of influence as you go through life. Use this as a metric—how does this directly affect me? Do I have any control in/over this situation? If so, how can I respond productively and actively? If not, how can I ensure this doesn't have an impact on me or my mental health?

Meditation and Connection with Resilient Plants and Animals

We have a whole host of plants and animals in the ecosystem around us who are masters of resilience—and we've met a few already: Raccoon, Japanese Knotweed, and Dandelion. Every ecosystem has these plants and animals: those cunning animals and resilient plants who can grow and thrive even in difficult circumstances.

Choose a plant, tree, or animal that speaks to you and who has some of the qualities of resilience you would like to cultivate, then work with that plant or animal however you see fit. If at all possible, spend time with that plant or animal; observe and see how they respond to adverse conditions. Work to bring that energy into your own life through reflection, through energy exchange (if permitted with the plant/animal), and by working to cultivate these same qualities in your life. If the plant offers, carry a piece with you.

One of the resilient plants that I often look to for guidance is the Staghorn Sumac tree (*Rhus typhina*) in my bioregion. Staghorn Sumac is extremely resilient, often able to grow in places that have been disrupted. Where I live in western Pennsylvania, Staghorn Sumac often grows along the edges of roads, persisting even after spraying and heavy chemical use. I had a wonderful mature patch on the edge of my property, and my neighbor cut the patch down, literally bulldozing the whole patch with a tractor, ripping the trees out by the roots, about four years ago. I mourned this patch and harvested some of the wood to honor and work with as an artist . . . and then joyfully watched the patch regrow. Now, the entire patch is back—all that the disruption did was make the patch grow back with more strength and power. When I am feeling like I need the qualities of resilience, I sit with this patch of Staghorn Sumac, who has so strongly rebounded after such a major disruption. I leave an offering for the gifts and lessons that Staghorn Sumac teaches. Since Staghorn Sumac is edible, I often will harvest the flower buds for a sumac drink as a magical aid in cultivating resilience, and I also carry a piece of the wood with me. This is an example of working closely with a plant teacher to cultivate resilience.

Contrary to what broader culture tells all of us, you are not a broken person; you are a strong person. You are part of nature, and therefore you have resilience in you, just like Raccoon and Japanese Knotweed. Each of us can flow with the strength of these powerful beings and our resilient ancestors.

Story of the Future:

AN ABUNDANT WORLD

After the low point where biological life and human societies were threatened with extinction, massive efforts are taken on every level: by individuals building refugia and relearning Baseline Ecological Knowledge, teaching these skills in their broader communities, creating alternative economic systems of gifting and barter, and reindigenizing to sustainably meet our needs in our local ecosystems.

Local communities have come together to protect and preserve land in their immediate ecosystem, including regional organizations who work to identify critical areas to protect, preserve, and expand, and larger nonprofit organizations and NGOs globally who establish migration corridors. Governments, pressured by their people, set aside enormous tracts of land to rewild with no management, tear down dams, protect waterways from overfishing, and create massive incentives to protect life. Billions of trees are replanted to sink the carbon produced in the twentieth and early twenty-first centuries. And most importantly, humanity takes a long, hard look at the qualities that they want to cultivate to protect and nurture this beautiful planet—we turn away from greed, efficiency, and growth at all costs and embrace our role as caretakers, healers, and tenders of this beautiful land.

Our botanical medicinal plant sanctuary in Ohio has continued to grow throughout the twenty-first century . . . this original sanctuary, and the thousands of sanctuaries from it, were the seeds of a new revolution within human society. These seeds sprouted, grew, and eventually became one of the driving forces of change and protection. They now form a huge ecologically protected area that takes up almost half the state, with people working in local and regional ways within the sanctuary to grow medicinal plants, tend ecosystems, and practice the core values of earth and people care.

And all this hard work pays off on both a local and global level. By 2100, rather than seeing the world die, as most early-twenty-first-century projects suggest, the world is more abundant than ever—waterways are full of fish, huge tracts of land are permanently preserved to be left alone for life to flourish, and humanity has gotten their greed and narcissism under control. An emphasis on local community has replaced the push for globalization and monoculture, and now, all life—human and nonhuman—flourishes again.

DRUID
Enchantment, magically responsive world, life as ceremony
OVATE
Cultivating wonder, intuition, body radar, tracking omens & augury
BARD
Storytelling & reweaving the mythic threads, bardic circles, songs of the land
Reenchantment
Magic
Wonder
Intuition
Mysticism

CHAPTER 6

Reenchantment

With Nate Summers

Story of the Past:

THE DISENCHANTMENT OF THE WORLD

Once upon a time, the world was enchanted. Magic was a way of life, and humans, nature, and the unseen thrived. No, this is not the beginning of a fairy tale or a fantasy story with dragons and unicorns; rather, this is a description of the way things were and in some cases still are in places around the world.

A magical, mystical worldview of nature filled with all sorts of noncorporeal beings has been a dominant perspective in nature-based cultures for untold millennia. People had magical connections to unseen spirits and mysterious forces. They wielded sacred powers linked to the elements and nature, and somehow people and nature thrived in some of the harshest conditions on the planet from the Arctic to the Kalahari Desert.

Lakota medicine men and women conducted seven sacred ceremonies to rejuvenate the people, nature, and spirit. The Anishinaabe were giving a sacred Tent Shaking ceremony to enable people to directly communicate with the spirits of nature and the spirit world in order to bring healing, harmony, and health to the people and nature. Daoist and Shinto priests of East Asia conducted ceremonies at ancient ceremonial shrines, ensuring the harmony among humanity, the natural world, and the spiritual cosmos. South and Central American Ayahuasqueros and Curanderos tended to the needs of people, place, and spirit through extremely elaborate and sophisticated plant medicine ceremonies. Siberian and central Asian shamans wove together song, trance states, spirit communication, and healing work to keep their people alive in a fierce landscape by aligning with the spirits of everything. South Asian spiritual leaders led people in ancient Vedic ceremonies, including fire puja to unite people, the gods, and nature. Australian Aboriginal tribal groups live in vitalized, dynamic landscapes brought to life through a combination of story, song, ceremony, and spirit known as Songlines, manifestations of the ancient state of oneness known as the Dreaming. In pre-Christian Europe, powerful spiritual ceremonies were conducted in sacred groves of ancient trees in order to unite, heal, and harmonize people, nature, and the unseen. And, in perhaps the oldest ceremonies in the world, San Bushmen medicine men and women conducted all-night trance-dance spirit ceremonies to bring everyone back to an original state of oneness with nature. Belief in an inherent energy that moves through all things, a spirit world that is a vital part of life, and the sacred role of humans as caretakers and nourishers of nature and the natural world was nearly universal.

In the sacred lands of the Pacific Northwest, also known as Cascadia, sacred spirit beings known as Changers came and shaped the landscape. Creating mountains, waterfalls, rivers, valleys, giant trees, and more, powerful guardian powers such as Coyote, Moon, Stellar's Jay, Turtle, and others shaped the world and imbued it with magic, story, energy, and vitality.

The people were animals and the animals were people. They spoke to one another and learned from one another continually. Song, dance, and ceremony were normal parts of life, as people used their sacred magic and powers to nourish and caretake the land, helping cocreate vast abundance. The rivers were packed with Salmon People several times a year, who, in a sacred reciprocal relationship, offered themselves up as food to the People, and the People responded by making sacrifices and ceremonies to the Salmon People in order to maintain the special covenant. Food and resources were plentiful for everyone.

And then things changed . . .

Strangers came in vast numbers. They brought with them new ways, new ideas, and new tools and technologies. At first they were welcomed in a traditional manner. But soon it became apparent that they took without giving back to the People or the land or the Animal Nations. They were possessed by an insatiable hunger, and they began to consume the land, the trees, the salmon, the otter, and more. Salmon became salmon. Cedar became cedar or just wood. The world was disenchanted. It became harder to follow the traditional ways, and eventually almost impossible, as people were forced off their land and the land was consumed all around them.

The world changed in ways it hadn't since the time of Changers.

The strangers forbid the old ways, the old ceremonies. The land, trees, and animals began to wither and decline as consumption without reciprocity or ceremony became the norm . . .

The Outsiders came and told people not to believe the old ways or they would go to hell. They were threatened, cajoled, and eventually killed if they disobeyed. Medicine women and men were hunted down and forced to give up their ways or die. Wise men and women (and especially those who didn't fall into either traditional gender category) were discredited, shamed, and sometimes literally burned alive. Give up your traditional views of the world or die. The people suffered. The spirits suffered. Nature suffered.

Later, a new round of people with another set of beliefs showed up. They didn't want you to believe in their God; they wanted you to believe that spirits didn't exist. There's nothing but stuff and things, and you should actually stop using all of your handmade, sacredly harvested items for your livelihood and use their artificial, cheap stuff instead. Soon machines came and replaced traditional ways of doing things. Whole cultures, peoples, and languages were destroyed, and the relationship among people, nature, and spirit was broken in a fundamental way.

The biosphere began to erode, slowly at first, and then more and more rapidly as the world became disenchanted . . .

It might be hard to believe, but there is almost a direct correlation between the adoption of a scientific-rationalist-materialist worldview and the rapid destruction of the biosphere. This is the belief that the world is made only of atoms, molecules, chemicals, and other forms of matter. Life and existence is random and doesn't have inherent meaning, and humans are the only ones to have ever developed significant levels of consciousness. This is the pervasive view of most forms of science, and it is in direct contrast to the experience and perspectives of cultures deeply embedded and connected with nature for hundreds of thousands of years. Ironically, scientists are now consistently trying to use science to stop global climate change. This is not to say that science is bad or that it doesn't have a place in the world. Clearly it does, and clearly it can and does help people out in specific situations and settings.

However, very little work has been done looking specifically at the rate at which people have destroyed the planet, and the connection with this behavior and our loss of belief in magic or the unseen. While one could argue that this was starting to happen for centuries, through the period of the Enlightenment in Europe, it is clear that in the late nineteenth century and the early twentieth century, through the rapid industrialization of much of the world and the corresponding rise in the belief that nature has no soul and there is no such thing as Spirit or spirits, that humanity's destruction of the natural world accelerated at an absurd pace, causing over two-thirds of the planet's natural areas to effectively disappear in just over one hundred years.

As we make our way into the still relatively early parts of the twenty-first century, this destruction continues at an unprecedented pace, even as scientists try to use scientific arguments to stop us from completely consuming the biosphere. But few, if any, are willing to point out that in times and places where people had or have a worldview of nature as a magical, alive, enchanted place, this kind of behavior simply did not happen. And in the few places left where this worldview is prevalent among humans, such as in remote tribes in the Amazon or among the few groups of African Bushmen tribes still following traditional ways, a magical worldview and a harmonious relationship with nature and the biosphere exist hand and hand. A view of the world as an enchanted place, one in which humans have an active part in cocreating reality with all the elements of nature and with spiritual forces, is one that actually promotes harmony, connection, and relationship.

After all, it's hard to cut down the forest if it's full of your friends. It's considered a bad idea to poison the river, if it's inhabited by a goddess. And surprisingly, traditional medicines, ceremonial ways, and sacred practices all still work and weave the connection among humans, nature, and spirit that has always been there.

It's time for us to reenchant the world and reweave the connections among nature, humans, and spirit. We invite everyone to believe in magic, spirit, and the unseen as we actively look for and embrace an enchanted world: one brought alive through our magical relationship with it.

Reenchantment as an Ovate

WONDER, AWARENESS, COMMUNICATION, AND TRACKING

Nature has often been considered the most magical of places, both in actual, living historical cultures and in the world of stories as well. Beginning to see the magic in nature is a key step in Reenchanting the world, but first a brief word of caution. There is a very fine line between a magical view of the world and delusion. There is a similar fine line between superstition and what we might call the supernatural, or perhaps more appropriately super-natural. It can be hard with our modern minds to look at nature and the natural world with magical eyes without our skepticism rearing its head. As we slowly move away from this view and find more of an animistic, spiritual, and connective relationship with nature, a lot of powerful and mysterious things can happen. However, we don't suddenly have to believe in unicorns to have a more magical relationship with nature (though who knows—that might actually help!). As we look at Ovate studies and reenchantment, it becomes rather easy to find the magic inherent in nature. Let's find the enchanted, magical threads of life out in nature and all around us.

Finding Wonder and Joy in Nature

My wife, Karen, has a wonderful practice she learned from a mentor of hers that is all about finding wonder in nature. It's accomplished mostly by wandering and paying attention in a relaxed, fun, and easy way. Often, when she takes the time to do this she makes the most-amazing discoveries and has stunning encounters. This can include everything from coming upon an ancient, old-growth tree, spotting a wild coyote, or discovering an animal skull in the ground.

While it might be easy to dismiss such experiences as coincidence or as attributing meaning to something that doesn't have inherent meaning, such a mindset misses the point. I remember hearing about this in an anthropology class in college, where we were looking deeply at magic in different Indigenous cultures. There was a famous story about an anthropologist who had the realization that the hunter-gatherer people he was with of course understood things such as physics and science in their own way; they just happened to ask the question "Why?" a lot more. The answer to the "why" was where the difference lay. If a sacred object falls off the wall and breaks, of course it was because the wind blew in suddenly. It's not as though people didn't understand that the wind caused the object to fall. But in the traditional culture, there was a deeper question of why did the wind blow at that moment and what is the message there.

If we go seeking wonder in nature with an open mind, heart, and body, we might be startled at the discoveries. If we have started to embrace an animist worldview, then we may suddenly find that a lot of things want to communicate with us. This may be really direct, but it is likely to start more subtly. Here are a few exercises to try:

- Wander with a sense of timelessness (more on this below).
- Pay careful attention to thresholds, especially where and when you enter a new part of the natural world. If you treat them as doorways or entrances by pausing and sensing permission to enter, you may find that a whole other world starts to open up for you.
- Look for "portals": unusual formations of rock, vegetation, or trees that look like something that longs to be stepped through. See what happens after you go through a portal in a respectful manner.
- Watch for sudden clues or signs along your journey, such as feathers, bones, skulls, the appearance of unusual animals, and more. Pay careful attention to what you were thinking about or what was going on when such a sign makes its appearance.
- Take on a playful, childlike mindset while doing all the above. It may actually be helpful to take a child under ten with you!
- Embrace the inherent joyful quality in all the above. Feeling delighted, full of wonder, and connected is actually a normal human experience when in nature.

Body Radar, Intuition, and Indigenous Feats of Awareness

Inherent in our body there is a deep knowing that directly connects us to nature and its inhabitants. While this ability may ultimately turn out to have a scientific explanation, currently it is one of the more magical abilities documented by humans in different times and places. Similar to how birds can navigate thousands of miles or salmon can find the very stream they were born in after spending years in the ocean, humans have the ability to find things with their body in an unexplained way.

Sometimes described as body radar or a form of body intuition, this phenomenon is most often found in hunter-gatherer people, usually with nomadic tendencies, though there are also stories of people having this ability in other closely connected nature cultures. Two of the most famous examples are from disparate parts of the world.

In *Original Wisdom*, author Robert Wolff shares multiple examples of how the Indigenous people of Indonesia whom he meets and works with have unexplainable abilities to find and discover things in the forest just by following an *inner pulling and knowing in their bodies*. Perhaps the most startling example is how the people he works with repeatedly know he is coming, and show up to greet him well before he is at their village, with no foreknowledge of his visit. Somehow they just arrive without any message being sent ahead. When he interviewed and pursued what was going on with his Indigenous hosts, they repeatedly pushed off the questions, insisting that this was something everybody inherently developed when growing up in the jungle.

The same phenomenon has been documented by multiple anthropologists and visitors among the San Bushmen and similar tribes (as related in books such as *Ropes to God* by Bradford Keeney and Paddy M. Hill). Furthermore, the San and others seem to be able to track game, find animals, and find plants and water through a similar method. This is documented in the films *The Great Dance* and *The Animal Communicator*, both directed by award-winning director Craig Foster, the director and creator of the Netflix film *My Octopus Teacher* (ironically, Craig Foster displays this same ability underwater with his octopus companion).

This ability to use our body to directly tap into the subtle energies in nature is not fully lost, nor is it exclusive to Indigenous hunter-gatherers in far-off locales or ancient times. It's something that can be cultivated and activated in all of us. Learning to activate, tune in to, and trust your body radar or body intuition is not as hard as it sounds, though it definitely takes practice and persistence. The simplest way to activate and strengthen this ability is to start to pay attention a lot more to your gut urges, body instincts, and natural inclination to go a certain way, especially in nature.

Now, of course, you need to do this responsibly and not simply start wandering off-trail anywhere and everywhere and either getting hopelessly lost or at the very least doing damage to the local ecosystem. However, in open areas that you are familiar with, you can start to tune in to your gut and let it lead you. You will probably be quite surprised by what you find. One way to activate this skill is to start your wander / body radar experience by pausing, connecting to your body, connecting to the place you are, and then actively putting your awareness into your navel or lower abdomen and tune in to the sensations you feel there. As you begin your wandering, regularly pay attention to that place in your body and even pause to bring your attention and awareness back there.

What do you feel? Do you feel pulled in a particular direction? Do you notice sensations in your lower abdomen or other areas as you are walking? What or where does this lead you to?

You can take this to the next level by actively picturing something in your mind or asking to find something. For instance, let's say you want to harvest some Stinging Nettle. You can ask the landscape where you can find a good patch to harvest from (there's some nice asking- and seeking-permission opportunities here as well), and then you can follow your gut to the nettle patch. You can do something similar by picturing a bird or animal in your mind that could be nearby, then body-wandering to find it. Instead of the actual animal, don't be surprised if instead you find its tracks, scat, skull, feather, or some other sign.

Why and how exactly humans have this capacity is a mystery. It may be a scientifically based dormant ability in our nervous system, but regardless, once you try it out and unlock the capacity, it becomes truly magical in helping you enter and interact with nature in a new way.[33]

Here are some key points to remember and to help activate this ability:

- This is an inherent, ancient human skill that everybody can learn.
- It helps to pause and be still at the beginning of your wander/exploration.
- Bring your awareness into your legs, feet, and lower abdomen. Pay attention to any sensations there.
- As you move, bring the attention back there periodically, paying particular attention to any sensations of pulling or being drawn in a certain direction or to a particular area.
- At the same time, allow your body to guide you and lead you where you are going.

- As you go deeper with this skill, you can ask your body to help you find a particular object or item such as an animal, track or sign, plant or tree, fungi, or natural feature. (It seems that for a lot of people, finding water this way is really accessible.)

Deepening Plant and Tree Communication

Around the world in closely connected nature communities, it is well understood that people can talk to and learn from plants and trees directly. We began exploring these connections in chapter 2, "Respect," and we deepen them here now.

Perhaps the most well-understood and well-documented version of this is illustrated with the *ayahuasquero/vegetalismo tradition* of South America,[34] where medicine people have been directly talking to plants and trees for millennia. In particular, the story of how people discovered the way to brew the potent sacred medicine of Ayahuasca itself from two different plants illustrates the point directly.

Each of the two main plants used to brew Ayahuasca has very different capacities and is relatively innocuous by itself. One of the two is extremely high in DMT, the natural molecule that is a powerful entheogen unlocking spiritual experiences. (DMT is produced naturally in the human body on its own. This may or may not be linked to other human spiritual experiences.) However, the DMT is not accessible to the human body because it cannot enter the bloodstream and reach the brain if the plant is consumed by itself. However, if the second plant is used in combination with the first, it *inhibits* the destruction of DMT in the digestive system and allows the DMT to enter the bloodstream and reach the brain, producing powerful, revelatory spiritual experiences. The plants do not grow together and are not botanically related.

So, how did people discover the way the plants work together synergistically? *The plants told them.*

At least that is the story the Ayahuasqueros tell about how they learned to make the sacred brew of their tradition. Going deep into the world of Vegetalismo is probably not the path for everyone reading this book, but taking a dive and starting to talk to trees and plants to find out what they have to say can be an incredibly rewarding and enlivening experience.

While it is true that plants and trees and their spirits may choose to communicate to us about many different things (for instance, one of my friends received a ceremony from a cedar tree), generally they are interested in telling us about how and what they can be used for. Often this falls into the category of medicinal, edible, and craft uses. You can find out more about how and in what ways they tend to communicate later in this book, but first an important word. *For this book's purposes, we should verify any and all plant uses independently through field guides, databases, and other reliable sources.* While the above statement might fly right in the face of what this chapter is all about, until you master this skill or unless you grew up in an intact ecologically connected culture and have been doing this your whole life, it's best to verify your experiences with other sources!

Okay, all that being said, don't be afraid to talk directly to the plants and trees in your area. But just like meeting new people, it can be rude to just go right up and start talking to somebody you just met. Like we mentioned in chapter 2, the foundation of connecting to the voices of nature is Respect. So start there. But also, over time, once relationships have been established, it is possible to ask trees and plants what they do or are useful for. You can do this out loud or silently. Everyone will tend to do this slightly differently and will get different information back. If you are a very visual person, you may want to use images to communicate, or you may get images back. If you are very kinesthetic, you may get embodied feelings back and forth. You may receive auditory feedback as well. Take note of what happens, keep a journal, and proceed steadily. You may be startled at what happens. This is a great precursor to making offerings to trees and plants and is also a great way to establish a relationship before harvesting.

Also, one thing you may want to do is to start with a familiar species or one that you *already know* its medicinal, edible, and ethnobotanical uses. This is a safe and smart way to start before reaching out to new friends.

Tracking Synchronicities, Omens, and Augury, and Communicating with the Intelligence of Nature

Have you ever had a dream come true? Have you ever been thinking about an old friend, and then out of nowhere they suddenly text you? Have you ever been thinking or talking about an animal and then suddenly see it?

All these kinds of experiences are examples of synchronicities—those odd moments when the external universe seems to line up with our own internal process. Almost everyone has experienced synchronicity, and a lot of people report that their synchronicities are enhanced and more frequent during intense life circumstances, when viewing the world through a magical lens, and with lots of time in nature.

Now, not every single animal encounter or sighting is necessarily deeply symbolic and important. Sometimes an eagle is just being an eagle. However, when you start to see the world as more magical and enchanted, often there is a big jump in synchronicities. For instance, you might be talking about a particular flower that you had a dream about, and then a friend brings you that flower, curious about what it is and how to identify it. Then later, you come across a patch of those flowers that you've never seen before. It's as if the universe is suddenly thrusting that flower into your life to be noticed. It can be really helpful to keep track of these moments, and also to ask ourselves the bigger question: "What is this trying to tell me?"

Ancestrally and in many modern-day nature-connected cultures, there is considered a consciousness or intelligence in nature that is constantly communicating with us. Often it communicates indirectly through dreams, signs, and symbols, including through external symbols in nature. Learn to watch for this, pay attention to it, and track it. Track the synchronicities, journal about them, and watch where they lead. As you do so, the magical world of nature will become more and more obvious.

As you'll read more about below, nature-connected cultures and peoples also often look for omens in nature and even ask questions directly to nature. The answers can sometimes be crystal clear and obvious, and sometimes a little bit more indirect. But in order to have this process work well, you need to be paying attention and have already started to track the mysteries, symbols, and synchronicities that nature is offering you.

A Reenchanted world is one in which our story and the stories of the world around us are interconnected and mutually informing one another.

Story of the Present:

ENCHANTMENT AWAKENS

The mainstream world is dominated by a rationalist-materialist approach deeply based on an extractive economic worldview. Greed dominates, and the natural world and the biosphere suffer. Scientists offer multiple scientific arguments about how and why we should change our behavior, both for our own benefit and the planet, but the arguments are mostly ignored.

Magical, spiritual, and animistic thinking is actively suppressed at all levels of education and academia and in the business/work world. Meanwhile, our entertainment world is dominated by magical mythological themes as our suppressed natural desire for a magical life finds a way to creep into the world through media everywhere. Marvel movies with archetypal godlike beings who have magical powers and who must continually save the world have dominated the box office for over a decade. Close behind are stories of strange space wizards who wield lightsabers and are in touch with a mystical energy known as the Force. Giant blue aliens with animist and Indigenous roots offer ecologically themed adventures with another message of saving the world and start to challenge Marvel movies for dominance. Anime, sci-fi, fantasy, and magical storytelling are everywhere, from books to film to graphic novels.

Meanwhile, magical worldviews and thinking are still dominant in most nature-connected and Indigenous cultures. In clear contrast to the rest of the modern world, they are not only not destroying the biosphere but are actively living in a regenerative relationship and have been for hundreds if not thousands of years.

At the same time, a magical revival has been underway for at least the past hundred years, and earth-based contemporaneous spiritual traditions with magical worldviews such as druidry, Wicca, and other forms of neopaganism grow exponentially. People around the world are actively using magic and ceremony to help heal the damage done to the earth. Native cultures and Indigenous teachings are experiencing a revitalization as old ceremonies and new ceremonies are brought to life to help reestablish balance and harmony in the world. People are allowed to speak their own language and practice their own religion again. Daoist ceremonies have been revived after the cultural revolution. Worldwide interest in Ayahuasca and South American Vegetalista traditions rises rapidly. The Songlines are still present and preserved and have begun to be nourished by new generations. In the face of almost impossible adversity, the San Bushmen have preserved their way of life, which has existed for at least sixty thousand years. Their trance dances are still happening, and where they are happening, the people, the land, and spirit are still connected.

Has the Reenchantment of the world begun?

Traditional people of Cascadia have bided their time, being careful and cautious as they've kept their precious, sacred traditions and languages alive as best they could. Slowly, they've won back traditional treaty and fishing rights. They've gathered money and resources through casinos on traditional lands and put those tremendous resources directly into cultural-revitalization programs. Canoe traditions of visiting one another are revived. Sacred regalia is worn once again. Longhouses are rebuilt or restored. Sacred ceremonies are able to be held again.

Restoration projects and reintroduction of native species such as the Kokanee Salmon take place in local lakes, and dams that once blocked the runs of salmon are removed.

The Reenchantment of the world has begun, and people are remembering they are the People and start to realize that salmon are also the Salmon People.

Reenchantment as a Bard

STORYTELLING AND REWEAVING THE MYTHIC THREADS

The ancient art of storytelling, as well as poetry, song, music, and related arts, has always had an extremely close relationship with magic and enchantment. Even the word "enchantment" itself is related to music and magical sound. An enchantment originally meant a chant, song, or spoken spell that produced a magical effect in the world. As we seek to Reenchant the world, the path of the Bard and its related arts becomes rich, fertile ground from which to grow a new magical, regenerative view of the world and our role in it.

Storytelling as Magical Work

The book you are reading is based on and in fact was conceived around the idea that *stories matter*. In fact, to take it one step further (and this is a statement that most fields of academia would actually agree with), stories shape and create reality. There are two fundamental ways to understand this idea. One of these is that stories shape our belief (more strongly than we probably realize) and that as our belief changes, so does our experience of reality. However, a much-older, more profound, and frankly powerful esoteric idea is that stories actually shape and create reality *directly*. This can be a difficult thing to wrap our heads around, and when taken to an extreme, it can probably produce delusions in some people with mental health problems (for instance, no matter how many superhero movies you see, you're not going to start physically flying around). Yet, when we look at traditional cultures connected deeply to different landscapes, stories contain deep teachings that unveil and unlock a way of being in right relationship to land, place, ancestors, spirits, and more.

Right now, there are a few pervasive and deeply powerful stories being sold worldwide (but especially in America). One is that our reality is nothing but matter (with the implication that nothing actually matters), and that we have the right to do whatever we want to and with nature. Another pervasive story that is a particular zeitgeist (spirit story of this particular time) of the last decade or so is that of Dystopia and Apocalypse. This story basically says that we are doomed to a dark apocalyptic future and that we are powerless to stop it. We are destined to fail and live in a grimdark world where people treat each other and the planet terribly. Ironically, our living, real world continues to become more and more dystopian as we consume media where dystopia becomes the norm.

We have the power to tell different stories. We don't need to be ostriches in the sand and deny the reality of our moment, nor do we need to be a Pollyanna who wants to see only the good side of things. However, we can choose to tell different stories. Stories of heroic hope. Stories of triumph. Stories of the ancient past. Stories of a regenerative future. Stories of people who are currently doing good in the world.

As humans, we deeply, deeply long for stories. Our brains are actually designed to learn from stories, and stories are one of the oldest forms of education on the planet. Information and lessons from stories go directly into our subconscious brain, changing and altering our behavior for better or worse (the advertising and entertainment industries are acutely aware of this; it is the primary way they work and make money). We need to make ourselves consciously aware of this and look at the stories we tell ourselves, our children, and one another.

We need to tell a better story . . . and that is what all of us are beginning to do (and which we will help empower all of us to do, especially in our next chapter).

Catching Songs and Stories from the Land

In our modern day and age of high degrees of specialization, it can be pretty hard to realize that in many traditional cultures, everyone had artistic expression and contributions of some sort. Probably the best-known modern-day example of this is Bali, where in some of the jungle cultures you can still find people who are artists, carpenters, performers, storytellers, and ceremonialists all rolled into one.

As we think of Reenchanting our art and finding our own artistic expression, this question arises: "Where do songs and stories come from anyway?" While there is no single answer to this question, and there are probably several correct answers, in nature-based cultures, many of the stories and songs *come from the land itself*. In fact, this idea is hardly new. The ancient Bards of Wales, including the famous Taliesin, who wrote in the thirteenth century, recognized the "awen" as the source of all creative, divine inspiration flowing through nature. The idea that nature can be inspiration, and that nature can offer stories and songs to humans to bring into manifestation, is as old as time.

This may seem like a stretch for people who have grown up in a completely modern context. But I know several people and have experienced myself catching both stories and songs from the land. In fact, this tradition is not as far removed as you might imagine. While there are many stories and examples of people receiving songs from trees or plants or the land in another language—what is often called "vocalables"—several contemporary musical artists have also shared that they have received their songs from nature. In fact, Bill Munroe, "grandfather" of the bluegrass scene, deliberately went and caught songs from nature and from the wind. Bob Dylan talks of a similar process.[35]

Spending time in nature, wandering, doing Sit Spot, exploring, talking with the trees and wind, expressing gratitude, and making offerings starts to unlock a two-way door of communication and connection, and don't be surprised if a story or song makes its way to you as part of this relationship.

One idea here is that you can work to open yourself up as an intentional vessel for the spirits of nature to flow through you, to create songs, stories, artwork, and other creations from the living earth. Nature has so many things to share and so few people listening. For example, Dana routinely uses an approach where she goes out into the land to see what messages the spirits of nature want her to paint, write, or share with her broader community. She goes to a Sit Spot or other sacred place with her tools (a field box of paints, a sketchbook, a notebook for writing) and asks the spirits of the place, "What do you want to share? How can I share your story and song?" And then she opens herself up and lets the enchantment flow through her, the images, stories, and wisdom coming not from herself but from the living earth. Those creations end up being what she writes about on her blog and in her books, and what artwork she creates and shares more broadly.

How might you make this happen? There are lots of ways, but here are a few suggestions:

- Cultivating curiosity, wonder, and openness to the land and the world of nature makes you more open to catching stories and songs.

- Cultivating your inner listening and spirit communication techniques (as described in the "Respect" and "Rewilding" chapters)
- Honing your own skills (singing, writing, crafting, visual arts, songwriting) so that you are a worthy vessel and can bring into manifestation that which is offered
- Doing this work with a group of other people who are also seeking inspirations from nature and building community around these practices
- Having a lot of unstructured time in nature to simply be—to frolic, create, and see what happens

Singing to the Land

Previously we've discussed different ways of making offerings to the land and the land spirits where you live. Often when people think of giving something to the land (or the plants or a tree), they think of a concrete, tangible thing. Perhaps it's something you've made or prepared. Perhaps it's something that was offered traditionally, such as water, cornmeal, or tobacco. While these physical tangible forms of offering and reciprocity are very powerful, it is also possible to nourish the land, the spirits, and all the beings in nontangible ways as well.

The most obvious example is gratitude, and in some ways this may be the most powerful and effective of offerings. But there are teachings around the world that mention time and again that the plants, trees, and nature spirits love to be sung to. There may even be some strong scientific evidence behind this, since research has shown repeatedly that plants respond very strongly to music and especially thrive and grow extremely well when exposed to positive, uplifting music and sound. (The converse is true as well: Plants will wither and fail to thrive if exposed to dark, ugly, harsh music. This is documented extensively in the book *The Secret Life of Plants*.)[36]

To engage in this practice, you don't have to be a gifted musician or singer. Finding a way to use your voice to make an offering can be intimidating at first, and perhaps you can find a group of people who are more used to or comfortable with singing to sing to the land, the trees, the river, or the ocean together. However, sincerity here counts a lot more than talent (believe me, I know; I'm not very much of a singer). You can simplify the process by simply chanting different sounds with meaning to the land as well. It seems that the vibration and the intention behind it are the two most important parts.

Just keep in mind the teaching that this is deeply healing and nourishing to the land, to nature, and to the beings both seen and unseen who dwell there.

Living a Mythopoetic Life and the Hero's Journey

It seems that one of the greatest examples of modern malaise is the sense that life is meaningless. Similarly, people struggle with the idea that we are not living the life we are meant to live. I mean, are we really meant to spend all day, every day in front of flat, two-dimensional screens? Are we really meant to have most of our self-worth tied up in "likes" and "dislikes" from a whole bunch of "friends" and "followers" whom we never really see in real life? What if we are designed and destined to live lives filled with more meaning than that?

And if that's the case, how do we go about finding and following that life path? As you may have noticed, I find it strangely compelling that our modern stories and myths in the forms of films, books, and shows are so filled with magic, heroes, high adventure, excitement, triumph, tragedy, and people wielding magical or nearly magical powers. Is this telling us something? Is there a memory here trying to surface?

When the first movie in James Cameron's *Avatar* saga came out, people were so touched by the movie, its message, and the experience that a number of folks actually fell into an *Avatar*-induced depression. It was almost like the movie was trying to tell us that our lives could be more like the blue-skinned Navii, who spoke directly to animals, trees, and other beings of the forest; who rode wild beings through the skies of their planet; and who led a life free and at ease with the world around them but filled with excitement and adventure. Cameron has explicitly said that the Navii in both the first movie and its subsequent sequel (with more on the way) are meant to be a stand-in for Indigenous people and an Indigenous way of life.

Can we live a life filled with deeper meaning? Shouldn't we be living a life with deeper meaning? I recall a story I've heard passed down from Australian Aboriginal culture about a young man who had come of age and was ready to go on a rite-of-passage walkabout. He was getting ready to set out on a journey that was likely to last months, possibly a year or more. He wasn't quite sure where to start, and so he turned to the elders and asked, "Where do I start?" They replied, "With the stories and the song lines you've learned since you were young."

The young man followed their advice and headed first to a nearby rock that was sacred and an important part of one of their key stories. From there, he simply followed the story and songs of the land and eventually found his way to where he needed to go and made his journey.

My experience has been, over decades of working with people from all walks of life, that we all are longing for deeper meaning, answers to life's big questions, rites of passage, elders and mentors to set us on a journey, and heroic adventures along the way.

You might say that we all long for a Mythopoetic life—a life filled with story, meaning, message, and an opportunity to set out on quests, make our own discoveries, and bring about deep wisdom, knowledge, and understanding for ourselves and our people.

You can see this practice woven into the deep traditions of the vision fasts or quests of Native North America, the Ayahuasca *dieta* plant fasts and retreats, and even the sitting out (*utiseta*) and quest traditions of Europe.[37]

How can we possibly live a life in this way in modern times? Here are a few suggestions:

- Actively seek and search for wonder and meaning in time in nature.
- See small and large journeys into nature as part of the larger story of your life and the opportunity to bring back lessons and wisdom.
- Cultivate relationships with friends, mentors, and elders who will support you in these processes and who will see you off and welcome you back after these kinds of trips.
- Take deep questions out into the wild and wait for the answers.
- Track the answers and synchronicities as the deep wisdom and intelligence of nature communicates back to you through signs and symbols—journal this and look for the deeper meanings.
- Find the magical in the ordinary.
- Deliberately cultivate a community of like-minded people following the deeper truths of their lives.

Bardic Circles and Reweaving the Mythic Threads

As I've begun to share in some of these practices above, hearing the stories and songs of the land and being inspired by nature is only part of the equation. The other part is learning to share that with each other, to hold space for each other, and to build community around those practices. This is where the bardic circles (called Eisteddfod in Wales and in some parts of the Druid tradition) can be helpful. This concept is as old as time—people coming together to share stories, songs, and messages from nature around the fire. The modern Druid tradition does this very well—almost any time a group of Druids gather, they hold an eisteddfod or bardic circle. A fire is built, and people come to the fire to listen to each other, support each other, and be inspired or entertained. Some people prepare material in advance, practicing for months and creating new material to share—stories, skits, music, poetry, and more. Others are inspired in the moment and perform spontaneously. Everyone is supported as they perform, regardless of how long they have been honing their skill. In fact, sometimes the most-beloved offerings are those that are silly, outlandish, and highly entertaining. You can start a simple bardic circle with friends—invite everyone over for a potluck and a fire and ask everyone who is willing to bring a story, song, or poem to share. Ask people to bring instruments and play music around the fire, enjoying the setting of the sun and the rising of the moon. Recognize that we've been doing this for tens of thousands of years, and feel that reenchantment weaving within.

Reenchantment as a Druid

AN ENCHANTED SPIRITUALITY

As we shift our lens to the world of the Druid, it is not too hard to bring magic into the equation. After all, we are looking at the Druid path and lens as the source of cosmology, ceremony, meditation, and magic itself. Both the Druids of old and the Druids of now are inextricably linked with magic and literal enchantment. Perhaps the most important aspect of Reenchanting is the actual bringing back of magic and a magical worldview.

Cosmology: An Enchanted, Magically Responsive World

In his work *The World We Used to Live In*,[38] Native American author, scholar, and activist Vine Deloria Jr. shares dozens of stories of the power of Native medicine people that took place just a generation or two ago. In these stories, it is normal and regular for holy people to make major changes in the weather; to produce radical, miraculous healing; and to help the land regenerate, rejuvenate, and grow. This is not considered impossible; it is considered normal. Not to mention that these same holy people are talking directly to nonhuman spirits, trees, plants, and animals.

For many people, these are just stories, lies, and fabrications at worst and delusion or exaggeration at best. But the reality is that most (if not all) earth-connected cultures believe that humans, when they are in an upright and holy relationship with the earth and the unseen, can literally change the world. This may be a shock for many or too much to believe, but I have something important to share. I've seen this myself dozens of times, and I am now utterly convinced that we humans have the ability to change our world in a powerful, positive way through magical acts. This effect is amplified dramatically with a group of sincere, like-minded people. I've personally witnessed people experience dramatic healings from highly traumatic car accidents, seen droughts end as water falls from the sky out of nowhere (with no rain in the forecast), seen sudden significant rainbows or double rainbows, and experienced very specific circular holes in thick rain clouds providing sunlight to fall upon the people conducting the ceremony.

I'll share a brief story: Just a few years ago, an area near my home that borders a lovely county park was clear-cut by a logging company. This was a shock to many, since it looked as if the company had actually cut right down into the park. In actuality, they had merely cut the land they owned, but many people didn't realize that the land was logging land to begin with. My wife and I were both frustrated and distraught, and besides taking civic action around what happened (phone calls, community discussion, working with the park), we were inspired to do a ceremony for healing the land.

On a Sunday afternoon, we hiked up to the clear-cut area with our toddler son. We separated, and each did our own very simple but sincere ceremony. We offered condolences and apologies to the land, prayed for its healing, and made simple offerings and blessings. While we were in the middle of each of our own mini ceremonies, a bald eagle flew directly up the ravine we were on the edge of, and called repeatedly.

To all of us, the eagle's appearance and calling out seemed a clear signal from the land and the local nature spirits. It seemed to indicate a simple message of "We hear you. Thank you!" While that eagle's appearance and the message would have been enough, as we wrapped up our ceremony and headed down the forested hill (the part that was still forested), more eagles came to join the first. By the time we had walked the short five-to-ten-minute walk down the hill, there were five eagles flying above us, calling out repeatedly.

I don't share this story lightly, and when sharing this kind of special experience, you run the risk of ridicule, disbelief, skepticism, and other mental energies that take away from it. However, everything I've shared with you is completely true. And yes, bald eagles do live near my home, and I have seen them literally dozens of times. However, I'm a professional naturalist with over thirty years of field experience, and I can tell you that I've never had five bald eagles circle over me and call out repeatedly like that.

Magic works. It's a key part of the process of Reenchantment. This whole book has been gradually revealing more and more tools (especially in the Druid section of each chapter) of how to start to practice this magical way of being. It all leads to Reenchantment (and eventually ReVisioning; see chapter 7) and to you. Let me share one more little secret: I'm pretty sure the whole natural and spiritual world is just waiting for you to reengage with it.

Divination and Augury

Another area of magical working that has been present with deeply nature-connected cultures and has a vital place in a Reenchanted world is the practice of reading the signs and symbols that nature is offering to us. Nature and the spiritual energy that resides there can be a helpful, communicative force that can support us on our path. There are two related but slightly different areas that can be explored with this approach. These are known as augury and divination.

Most people are not familiar with the word "augury," but most people are familiar with the idea or concept of omen. Augury is simply the ability to read the omens of nature. While there is certainly a scientific and naturalist aspect to this, such as watching bird behavior for signs of weather changes or the behavior that some animals display before earthquakes, there is also definitely a more mystical and magical side. For instance, it is almost a worldwide phenomenon in nature-based cultures that unusual behavior in birds, and in particular the appearance of birds out of place and at unusual times, is somehow an indicator of death, often of a person known by the person witnessing the bird. Watching, learning, and observing the patterns of nature can tell us a great deal about the world around us and continue to unlock an animistic relationship, including one with the greater intelligence of Nature itself. Noticing unusual behavior, things out of the norm, and strange happenings can tell us about what is happening in the natural world and the unseen world of spirit and mystery.

Divination is probably a term that people are more familiar with, though it is actually closely related to augury. Generally, divination involves asking a question, usually about the future, though not always, and the asking is usually done to an external set of symbols that are considered either an oracle or at the very least oracular. Popular and well-known divination tools include Tarot decks, the I Ching, runes, the Celtic Ogham, and more. Most cultures have multiple divination tools and devices. Looking deeply into these common examples of divination tools, it is easy to begin to see the deep-nature symbolism and signs that form the foundation of them. For instance, Ogham is a Celtic divination system primarily based on trees and plants. The runes are filled with symbols directly taken from nature, and the

I Ching too is filled with imagery and symbols from the natural world. In fact, Dana has developed multiple oracle decks from the trees and plants in nature that are powerful tools for answering questions, reflection, and meditation.

While using divination tools can be incredibly helpful and is certainly part of an enchanted and magical worldview, it is worth considering that one of the oldest forms of divination is simply taking a question directly to nature itself. Formulating a clear question, asking it out in nature, and then waiting for an answer is one of the most powerful and effective forms of divination I know. Often the answer appears in the movement or appearance of an animal, a certain shape noticed in water or clouds, or even spontaneous words or answers popping into your mind that seem to come from a tree, a mountain, or a river. It can take awhile to get a clear answer, and so it's necessary to cultivate patience and wait, but you also might be surprised at how quickly you get an answer back. It is probably clear now that if you practice augury and learn to read signs and symbols in nature, it is an incredible asset for when you start asking questions of nature directly through a divination practice.

Learning the ways of augury and divination, especially direct nature-based versions of both, greatly enhances your relationship with nature as a form of divine intelligence and inspiration. It is a helpful step in discovering a Reenchanted world.

Meditation and Enchantment

Throughout this book, we've offered several meditations, but they have often been of a different flavor and sort from what most people think of as traditional meditation: sitting quietly, inside, and stilling the mind. There is nothing wrong with those traditional approaches. They are quite effective and helpful, but once again in this chapter we will look at something else. As we embrace the ideas of a Reenchanted world and a magical worldview, similarly our meditations can have a magical and enchanted flavor and feel.

Learning to see and visualize the world as healed, healthy, and regenerated is a powerful form of meditation and magic. Here the world of dreams, visions, and our waking reality blends together. Taking just five minutes a day to visualize and see strongly in your mind's eye a regenerated biosphere and healthful human-nature-spirit interaction can be a very effective meditative practice with powerful results in the world. This is not as easy as it sounds, and if you are able to build up your ability to meditate in this way to ten minutes or twenty, the power amplifies. Of course, it is also easier sometimes to focus on a smaller area (say, our local neighborhood, town, or city, or the watershed we are a part of). Here is a way of incorporating this powerful magical tool into a daily practice:

- Sit in a comfortable seated posture that you can stay in for at least ten minutes. Use pillows or a blanket to assist if necessary (and yes, this practice can done outdoors).
- Begin by breathing in a relaxed manner for at least ten breaths (eyes can be partially open for this part).
- Visualize roots extending from the base of your body into the ground. Breath gently and naturally. Next, visualize the core, spine, and trunk of your body as the trunk of a tree. Continue to breathe in a relaxed and easy manner. Finally, visualize branches extended from the crown of your head up into the sky and heaven above (you can have eyes partially open for this if it's helpful).
- Spend at least a couple of minutes just breathing and being comfortable in this visualization and posture.
- Next, with your eyes closed, visualize in your mind the natural world as regenerated, healed, restored, and in harmony. Start nearby and let your mind's eye paint the picture and extend the imagery as far as is comfortable (again, when first doing this practice, start small). Hold the image gently in your mind's eye in a comfortable way. If your mind drifts, that's fine. Just gently bring your awareness back to the imagery.
- After doing this for a few minutes (and no more than five to start with), gently release the image. It can be helpful to imagine the image traveling up and out of your body. But this isn't necessary.
- Return to the tree meditation. Gradually allow that to dissolve.
- Slowly open your eyes and gently rub your body from head to toe. It may be good to eat or drink something.

Note: This is a practice that gradually builds potency and power. It is best done consistently in small amounts over a long time, slowly adding time and clarity. Over time, this practice will gradually help bring into your life what you visualize. It can be healing both for people and nature and strongly strengthen your ability to make the world around you a better place.

Reenchantment: Life as a Ceremony

One of the major threads weaving through this book is that ceremonies have power: the power to change the world, and the power to build a better vision for the future and nourish all life on this earth. We will note that most modern cultures are devoid of meaningful ceremonies, and this lack of ceremony breeds disenchantment. A balm and restorative exercise both for you and the living earth is building in ceremonies throughout your life.

We can illustrate the power of weaving ceremonies into life to combat disenchantment in two examples. In our first example, a person gets up, brushes their teeth, combs their hair, puts on their work clothes, and gets in their car. They stop at a drive-through before going to the office for the next nine hours. They come home, eat a takeout dinner, visit the gym, and then sit down for some entertainment before falling asleep. Imagine this person instead with a life full of ceremony. They still have the same routine and job but have made a conscious effort to build in a life of ceremonies. Thus, before they leave their apartment, they take fifteen minutes in the morning to observe the sunrise on their patio overlooking the city and to offer morning gratitude. At their lunch hour, they take their lunch into the park near their building, do some movement and walking meditation, and visit their Sit Spot, coming back from lunch refreshed and with new lessons from the local genius loci. After dinner, they meet with a group of friends to share stories and make some music together at a local community garden. Divination and quiet reflection before bed complete their day. While these individuals have the same job, same routine, and same life demands, one has built ceremony meaningfully into their lives and is living a much more enchanted and spirit-filled life—and that has tremendous benefit for themselves, their community, and the spirits of nature and the land where they live.

In this book, we've explored the basic building blocks of nature-focused ceremonies, which are meaningful, rich, and reverent while also being joyful, unscripted, and even impromptu. The book has explored how to build in ceremonial practices through offerings and gratitude, and we've deeply explored how to use ceremonies to bless and heal the land. These various ceremonial tools have several core functions. The first function is to help build and deepen the energetic threads between humans and the land. The second is to nourish the land, offering blessing, healing, and gratitude. The third is to nourish humans themselves, giving them grounding, meaning, and resilience in a challenging world.

Weaving these threads together, an enchanted view of the world is one where we take these basic building blocks and weave them firmly into our lives, as we see in the second example above. These ceremonies, formal and informal, at regular intervals, help build enchantment into our daily lives. Consider building small ceremonies into your routine of daily life. These ceremonies can be practiced daily or a few times a week. Here are some suggestions:

- Finding a Sit Spot and spending regular time in nature where you make offerings, listen to the stories of the land and communicate with the nature spirits.
- Using ceremonies to "bookend" your days: How will you start your day with ceremony? How will you end it? To do this effectively, examine the cycles and patterns of your life and find ways of directly building ceremonies into your day—even small ones that take only a few minutes. Simple nature observations, gratitude, meditations, protection, blessings, and small moments of connection all are powerful ideas here.
- Use your intuition to bring ceremony in as needed. Check in regularly with yourself and with the local land spirits to see what either of you are needing, and rewild ceremonies as you feel led.

Enchanting and Wild Crafting the Wheel of the Year

In addition to ceremony in daily life, to bring an enchanted ceremonial practice, you may also want to work to establish some regular cycle of ceremonies tied to seasonal changes in the land around you. This practice is as old as time and, to be rewilded and reconnected, can be local and specific to you. Please note that while many neopagan traditions use the eightfold Wheel of the Year, this may be appropriate only to temperate climates in certain northern latitudes. While you can use the Wheel of the Year for inspiration, it is better to adapt or wild-craft your own entirely. Here are some starting points examining the cycle of the sun and the cycle of the earth.

The cycle of the sun **is a universal constant on our planet**, and the solstices and equinoxes are ancient holidays celebrated by many peoples across time. Thus, regardless of what is happening on the earth, we can always use the path of the sun and the light in the world to observe the light of the sun and year. Thus, you can think about how you might meaningfully mark the times of greatest light (summer solstice) and greatest darkness (winter solstice), and the two days of balance (fall and spring equinoxes). How might you mark these in your own way, and how might you build community around these events?

The ***cycle of the earth*** **is where things become unique and specific to your ecosystem.** This yearly cycle of the land includes your specific climate, the waxing and waning of plant life, the patterns of animals and birds, the amount and nature of precipitation, when harvests happen, and key human cultural patterns—and of course, this is all dependent on where you live. One suggestion that has worked for many people looking to develop a deeper connection to the cycle of the earth is to use a Sit Spot and observe the changes in the seasons. Here's the basic practice:

- Dedicate time to this Sit Spot practice at least twice a week, when you are deeply observing the seasonal changes on the landscape. As you are out and about in the land around you, also observe what is happening.
- Keep some kind of record of your observations: photographs, videos, sketches, journal entries, so that you can think about your local seasonal wheel.
- In observing, note anything that changes: bloom times, snow melting, fogs rolling in, rains, acorns dropping, and so forth. The goal is to document what is happening in your ecosystem, so that you can identify any "seasonal shifts" that occur with regularity.
- Try to disavow yourself of the regular notions of "seasonality" (e.g., it is spring, so these things happen) and instead simply observe.

From these observations, pinpoint what you would consider meaningful changes in your ecosystem that may be cause for celebration and ceremony. For Dana, for example, the first flowing of the maple sap, the first blooming of the hawthorn and elderberry, the first snow, and the first hard frost all are moments that she uses to craft meaningful ceremonies to honor, bless, and mark the seasonal changes. From there, you can start to wild-craft your own set of seasonal celebrations that deeply embed you with the land around you and help you craft an enchanted spiritual life.

Story of the Future:
AN ENCHANTED LAND

Nature is no longer a place to go and simply extract whatever you think you need whenever you want. Rather, it is a magical place once again filled with spirits and beings that are communicated with and respected regularly that provides for everyone's needs. Ceremonies and offerings are made that nourish the people, the land, and the spirits. The biosphere has regenerated and rejuvenated. Stories and songs regularly arise and are shared with the land in a reciprocal loop of creativity. Dreams and visions are a regular part of everyone's lives. Medicine people of all traditions are celebrated and honored as specialists, but everyone's own inherent connection to nature, spirit, and people is woven into daily life. The spirits are happy, the land flourishes, and the people feel deeply, wildly human again. The world has been Reenchanted.

The Salmon People return in great number every year. The People are now all people, and they gather together to give thanks for the Salmon's return and offer ceremonies of reciprocity and rejuvenation. Similar work is done with the trees and forests, as the People work to regrow old-growth forests and cedar is now again Cedar. Wolves run wild in a free and sacred manner but are communicated in a way to allow them to travel where they need to while the People are safe and protected. The spirits of cities, towns, valleys, mountains, and forests are communicated with regularly, and in sacred dance, song, and ceremony the Animal People and others show up to talk with the People about what is or is not needed in the Great Dance of Life.

The Changer Spirits smile upon the People and the Land. The world has been Reenchanted . . .

Nature
Humans
Spirit
Biocentric Animism
Sharing the Vision
Bardic Visioning
Telling a Better Story
Broadening the Vision
A New Paradigm Emerges
Ceremonies as Earth Medicine
Reconnection
Respect
Rewilding
Regeneration
Resilience
Reenchantment
Revisioning

CHAPTER 7

ReVisioning

With Dana O'Driscoll and Nate Summers

Never doubt that a small group of thoughtful, committed citizens can change the world; indeed, it's the only thing that ever has.

—MARGARET MEAD

It is easy to underestimate the power of the above quote. Believe it or not, many of the biggest changes in our world and in our history came about from small groups of people working together toward a common goal to create change in the world. From women's suffrage, to recycling, to the banishment of segregation and apartheid, many of these movements have developed, grown, and then created a huge impact by starting with a small group of dedicated people creating the change in the world they wanted to see.

And this is not always benign. For instance, it's not really common knowledge that the consumer, throw-away society that we currently live in was actually a deliberate development created by a small group of people after World War II as a way to design the world they wanted.[39] The idea was to create a postwar economic boom that fundamentally redesigned how and what people consumed and when, and created a throwaway society (before that time many consumer goods were built to last a very long time, as much as a lifetime).

Another great example are our modern schools. While there can be a hearty and lively debate about the value of the modern education system, what can't be debated is the original design behind our elementary and secondary education system. The originators of the public education system were heavily influenced by the industrial revolution that was going on and the realization that there was a need for workers. Modern schools were designed (with bells and all) to prepare people to work in factories and serve the needs of the industrial revolution. A lot has changed since then, but the basic structure of school (how long, the number of breaks, the length of the school year) hasn't changed much. Also of note, the current school system also is designed to "free" parents up to work long days as well.

It's almost as if the world we are living in was deliberately made and designed to be a certain way by a small group of people with a **certain vision of how things should be.**

Ironically, a strong argument could be made that not only is there a powerful form of design, creation, and even manipulation happening, it is likely that something is happening on a more subtle, magical level as well.

For instance, did you know that it's incredibly common among the very wealthy to use visualization, visioning, goal setting, vision boards, and other semimagical means to create the ultra-wealthy, glamorous life they want? Originally offered by Napoleon Hill and other New Thought leaders and writers in the early twentieth century, this form of abundance and wealth magic is used by proponents of the abundance, wealth, and rich mindset including folks like Oprah Winfrey. Some of these same approaches and teachings were made popular in the movie *The Secret* as well. It's not a well-known fact that Donald Trump is a follower of New Thought approaches, and it could be argued that much of his continued success as a political figure is through his own unshakeable belief in his own story. So, if ultra-rich, wealthy, and powerful folks are using visioning and similar techniques to create the world we live in, why aren't the rest of us doing the same? Why can't we? Or are we and we don't realize it?

Many of us face the challenges of busy lifestyles, constant stimulation, lack of access, and lack of time and space to truly imagine a different and better world, let alone create it. We are bombarded by social media, news, and lots of other electronic sources that show us the world we are supposed to want where we consume and consume without ever questioning why or really understanding the impact on us or the world around us.

Late-stage capitalism has provided us with a series of visions about the future that are pretty terrifying. The grand narratives of infinite growth and progress at all costs have landed us in a warming age marked by the loss of biodiversity, climate instability, and growing social upheaval. Not many people feel positive about the future at present, but rather often express dread, fear, and anxiety. If we follow the present path of capitalism, it offers some pretty terrible visions of the future. The first vision it offers is that if we simply ignore the mounting warning signs, we basically consume the earth into a dystopian nightmare. As we explored in the Introduction, we have plenty of Hollywood blockbusters that share that particular vision. Another vision is that we somehow find a technological solution to the climate crisis (bioengineering, AI, etc.), and then are able to continue consuming. A third has to do with space travel—we find ways of mining the solar system's asteroid belt, and colonize Mars and the Moon and keep on consuming.

There's a pattern here: the visions of the future that late-stage capitalism offers are variations on a theme designed to keep the current growth and progress engines running through consumption and resource extraction of the living earth. How much of the earth has to be consumed and destroyed in order for these visions to end?

Can we envision a brighter, better future without this paradigm, instead using the themes outlined in this book: reconnection, respect, rewilding, regeneration, resilience, and reenchantment? In order to counter these narratives and in order to come into balance with nature culturally and globally, we need some new visioning, hopeful, positive, and balanced with the living earth.

Visions give us hope, they give us opportunity, and they ultimately help us make positive change. Before we can bring something into reality, we have to envision it. Visions become reality if enough people get behind them to make them happen.

Visioning is also a magical act—magic is all about setting our intentions, directing energy toward intentions, and then seeing a change in the world. Thus, visioning is a critically powerful opportunity to take meaningful steps to create a better world. The problem is that it seems that we have a stronger sense of the problems than the solutions—we know what is wrong, but we don't necessarily have a clear sense of what to do to fix it and create hope. So, the questions we have are: What does that vision look like? What are the specifics? Where do we find inspiration for that brighter vision of the future? Who creates these visions? Who enacts them?

It is our belief and hope that we can all undertake this work together becoming the small group (or very large group!) of dedicated people determined to make the world a better place by holding and manifesting a better vision of the future.

UNDERSTANDING THE RELATIONSHIPS OF THE 7 R'S

This entire book was written as a magical act—to empower you, to help bring forth a sacred vision to life, to help ensure the future of all life on this planet, and to offer a new paradigm for the present and future. Our chapters are carefully laid out as a journey. Our first R, Reconnection, gets us thinking about our relationship with the living earth and putting us into an actual relationship once more. Respect takes that a step further, describing what ethical interactions look like both with nature and with the world of spirits. These two chapters are our foundation for the rest of the Rs. We next moved into three adjacent approaches to deepening interactions with spirits, nature, and our human communities: Rewilding encourages us to recognize the inherent wisdom in nature, to see how nature can thrive without human intervention, and to explore our own inherent wildness. Regeneration takes the opposite approach, recognizing the incredible value when humans taking up their original roles as caretakers and work to undo the damage that has been wrought by human civilizations both within our human communities and for the living earth. Resilience offers yet another core set of tools, recognizing and cultivating the adaptability, creativity, and flexibility found both within us and in the living earth to navigate the present age. The Reenchantment chapter culminates in our end goal: getting us back to a world that is enchanted, full of spirits, nature, and life, as it once was for our human ancestors. Reenchantment is where we see these core connections of nature, spirit, and human come into their most healthy balance—where each is supporting the other. Reenchantment is why we have been telling this entire story—it offers a vision of how the world once was and could be again. If Reenchantment is the end goal, then this final chapter, ReVisioning, is the road map for how to get there. If we want that enchanted, sacred relationship of balance between the world of nature, the world of humans, and the world of spirit, we need the vision in order to proceed.

The Visionary Road Map of the 7 R's

Throughout this book, in addition to the written text, we've offered visionary artwork that created road maps for a healthy vision of the future—one example of using bardic practices for visioning, as we discuss in this chapter. Here are the visionary pieces of artwork we shared in each chapter:

- **Reconnection's** visionary road map depicts a healthy ecosystem and three kinds of webs: the spiderweb, the web of roots of plants and trees, and the mycelial web of life, emphasizing our connections to the world. The road map is lit by the Lightning

Bugs and features both Reishi and Mycena mushrooms. The sigil depicts our take on a Celtic endless knot, emphasizing that all beings and all things in existence are interconnected.

- **Respect's** visionary road map shares a gratitude mandala with White Oak and Chamomile, a plant and tree that have sacred and healing uses. The sigil is our take on a compass rose, allowing us to find our way back to respectful interaction with nature.
- **Rewilding's** visionary road map offers pathways of the Druid's symbol of the Awen (divine inspiration) being shaped through the tracks of many creatures. These tracks include bison, human, goose, and other animal trails—all leading together. Our sigil also reflects both those sets of tracks coming together as the sun rises and sets, and also represents the many faces of the creatures who live on our beautiful earth.
- **Regeneration's** visionary road map offers the future story depicted in the chapter—Clear Creek in a healthy ecosystem with the backdrop of the rolling hills in the Allegheny mountains. Our sigil depicts both the growth and healing that can come from regenerative practices as well as the cycles of life.
- **Resilience's** visionary road map shows a vision of an urban/suburban yard being converted to a front-yard garden ecosystem, brimming with life and abundance. This ecosystem offers habitat and creates a resilient opportunity to grow food and medicine, and provide for one's needs. The sigil features lines crossing, representing the many different resilient practices that can intersect, build, and meet the needs of both humans and nonhumans in harmony.
- **Reconnection's** visionary road map offers our take on the tree of life as depicted from the ancient Western alchemical texts, emphasizing the enchantment of the world and connecting the physical and metaphysical worlds in harmony. Our sigil likewise depicts the physical and metaphysical being joined again.

- **ReVisioning's** visionary road map offers the pathway to the future through the other six R's again using the visual flair from previous alchemical texts, moving from a place of destruction and human-caused death and suffering to a brighter and greener earth. The sigil is the triquetra or trinity knot, representing the unification and balance of humans, nature, and spirit.

- **Our Cover** offers another take on the alchemical-inspired graphic featuring the seven sigils in a sacred seven-star pattern surrounding a healed, vibrant, and green earth. The sun, moon, and planets, as well as the stars, surround our earth, demonstrating our connectedness to all existence. The goal of the cover is to show how a green, healed earth can be enriched with each of the 7 R's for a brighter future.

Each of these graphics offers examples of how the bardic arts offer a new kind of story and help vision the future. We offer both a magical symbol (the sigils) and approach each image from the desire to compliment and extend our words on the page. We've drawn upon the Western alchemical image tradition for the end results of the book: our cover, chapter 6: "Reenchantment," and chapter 7: "ReVisioning," representing the transformational process that must take place.

The magical process of creating these images took place after our book was drafted and included an initial discussion between Dana and Nate: Dana sketched drafts of the images and Nate developed an initial draft of each sigil. Once we were happy that the sigil and image was conveying the vision we wanted, Dana opened up a sacred grove (magical circle) in her art studio, set intentions, and developed each graphic with sacred intent. Thus, what we've provided here in this book is an example of using one form of the bardic arts to share the vision, as we explore further in this chapter by sharing an additional visual and magical layer to the text.

A TRIAD OF RELATIONSHIPS: NATURE, HUMANS, AND SPIRIT

Going hand in hand with all of the challenges of late-stage capitalism is anthropocentrism—the philosophical stance that places human life above all other life on earth and privileges humans and their needs. As we have deeply explored through the stories and the first six R's, most humans who live in modern, industrial, and technological societies have this human-dominated view, but it may be subconscious and is deeply woven into present human civilization. In this view, human life is seen as more important or valuable than other forms of life; humans have the right to do whatever they want to the earth, and choices are made based on what is best/most convenient to humanity. This results in at least three major problems that undercurrent the challenges we face today:

- Without an intrinsic belief in the value of all life, the earth is seen as a resource to extract. This view has created systems that have caused extensive damage and loss of life to happen and has ultimately resulted in the 6th mass extinction event taking place.
- Animals, plants, and other life are not given the same sovereignty or care given to other life; they are less important and their lives are less valuable. We can see this clearly in everything from the acceptance of medical testing on animals to factory farming animal operations.
- Humans are seen as somehow more highly "evolved" than other life and disconnected from it, and thus, deserving of more right to live and take up space than others, which has again led to the global predicament we now face.

Most modern humans living in industrialized nations often don't even recognize that they carry this anthropocentric perspective; it is just the way things are and have been, and it is subconscious or semiconscious. These beliefs run very, very deep and can impact every interaction and decision about nature and people's relationship with it. There appear to be many root causes of anthropocentrism, many of which we have explored in this book: capitalism, globalization, the myth of progress, colonialism, the rise of agriculture, monotheism, and domestication. While the above problems are serious, we have worked to present solutions through the first six R's—and this chapter, our final chapter, offers us the way to get there through ReVisioning.

What we have done in the last six chapters is to fight anthropocentrism and all of its resulting problems and work to move us toward a biocentric, animistic philosophy that interweaves connections to nature (ovate practices), the world of spirit (druid practices), and the human community (bardic practices). That is, we have presented our road map to a better future through exploring these interconnections in relationship to the core themes: reconnection, respect, rewilding, regeneration, resilience, and reenchantment. And while the "Bard, Ovate, and Druid" framework was useful for us to explore our core themes in the last six chapters, we also recognize that presenting them in such a way may minimize their interconnection. Thus, we deviate from this framework in our final chapter and show how nature, spirit, and humanity must be woven together. That is, if we are going to survive and create that better future for all life, humans need to connect not only to their local landscapes but also to the world of spirit once again. We can interweave these connections of our human communities with our relationships to all other persons on this planet that manifest through nature—and in doing so, create a space for all life to thrive.

Biocentric Animism

So how do we get there? What a healthy, balanced vision for the future might look like should include examining our role as human beings—specifically, in moving away from anthropocentrism (human-centeredness) and into cultivating balance and healthy relationships with the world of nature and the world of spirits.

Building from our discussion of animism in chapter 2, a first good step in the right direction is in **Biocentrism** and **Ecocentrism,** which offer more life-affirming views that recognize that humanity is but one of many forms of life on earth. **Biocentrism** places all life—the tree, the bird, the insect—at the same level as human life. This view recognizes that we are all equal and all deserving of life, and that humans need to recognize the sovereignty and right of all beings to live. **Ecocentrism** takes this a step further by placing the ecosystem and larger earth equal to human life, recognizing that the ecosystem as a whole has a right to sovereignty and life.

We know from ethnographic and historical research that many human cultures have held biocentric or ecocentric views and also lived in balance with their ecosystems. For example, in *Ropes to God: Experiencing the Bushman Spiritual Universe,*[40] Bradford Keeney describes the African Bushman tribe's innate connections with their surroundings. Keeney has a number of works on the Kalahari Bushman peoples, and they all are fascinating accounts of people who clearly recognize the equality of themselves and all life and who work to build spiritual connections to that larger world. We can see many more examples of these in Graeber and Wengrow's *The Dawn of Everything: A New History of Humanity*[41] (where they explore the concept of human freedom, among others).

In fact, the idea of a biocentric society is so threatening to anthropocentric cultures that Indigenous cultures were and still are often destroyed, eradicated, converted, and worked to be removed. Further, when scientists or Westerners often talk to or study individuals from these cultures, there is often the view that talking to nature spirits is somehow a metaphor rather than an actual practice. These ideas are ridiculed, dismissed, and laughed at—and yet they endure. Even when scientists name these beliefs, they identify them from a scientific, rationalistic standpoint and do not see the world of spirit—and this is where bringing together biocentrism and animism so important. Why does the world of spirit matter? As we learn from many Indigenous cultures and modern-day nature spirituality, the world of spirit matters because talking to the spirits of nature allow you to co-create intentions with nature (see "Reenchantment") and honor the sovereignty of beings by being in direct communication with them (see "Respect"). Without animism and spirit, nature remains voiceless and a mere object, rather than a subject, teacher, and mother. You can't enter a dialogue with the land to find out what the land needs—what visions, what ceremonies—if you refuse to acknowledge the spirits of the land. You can't learn the deep teachings of nature if you aren't able or willing to listen.

What is certainly present in the traditional cultures of the Kalahari Bushmen and other Indigenous peoples, is the threefold connection between humans, nature, and spirit. **Biocentric Animism** is that connection: it is the combination of biocentrism and animism: the world is not only full of incredible ecosystems and living, breathing beings, tucked into every corner of our beautiful planet and infinite in their variety, but that the world is enchanted and full of spirits. This view suggests that the challenges that we face as a species are not just physical and scientific problems but are also spiritual ones. These spiritual problems were present before the ecological problems occurred on a massive scale. These spiritual problems began with the disenchantment of the world and continued through colonialism and into the practices today. Hence why, as we explore in this chapter, visioning and ceremonies will have such power—because if we can solve the spiritual problem, we can be well on our way to solving the physical problems and adapting to the new realities we face. As the hermetic adage suggests, "As above, so below. As within, so without."

Shifting into a biocentric animist philosophy gets to the heart of this entire book: it is not enough to respect nature, to think nature is worth preserving, or to know a lot about nature; we need to see nature as an equal partner and live every day in cultivating that partnership with both the physical world of nature and her spirits. We need to co-create and co-vision the future with nature. This is why the synthesis of nature, humans, and spirit are so critical.

CEREMONIES AS MEDICINE FOR THE EARTH

As we began to explore in chapter 4: "Regeneration" and chapter 6: "Reenchantment," it was not that long ago (a generation or two) that people witnessed remarkable effects from ceremonies conducted in a traditional manner by ceremonial leaders in Indigenous and earth-based communities. Some of us may even have had the opportunity to experience that phenomenon still happening, especially in regard to miraculous "spontaneous" healings that sometimes occur for people through prayer, ceremony, and intention. Spontaneous remissions of cancer, remarkable sudden healing of heart ailments, healing of brain traumas, and so forth are just some of the extreme medical situations that have been recognized as miraculous healings.

What if the same thing could be done for the situation we are in with the land? What if we could conduct ceremonies to rebalance the climate, rejuvenate the biosphere, and restore the balance between humans, nature, and spirit?

It certainly seems as if the biosphere of the planet could use a miracle healing. What if, not only could we do such things, but rather we should be doing these kinds of ceremonies and they are actually one of the keys to ReVisioning the world and creating a brighter, better, future?

In several different contexts, with different teachers from Indigenous and earth-based cultures, Nate has heard wisdom keepers, medicine people, and ceremonial leaders share the following teaching (which Nate has paraphrased and which not only was Nate given permission to share, he was actually encouraged to share): "It's possible there will come a time in the future when earth changes start to become so powerful and strong that we will no longer be able to stop them through our physical actions alone. We will need to use ceremony and the spirits to reverse the process. It seems like we are coming close to that time or are already there. . . "

At the same time, we also see strong movements within the nature spirituality community that are focusing on larger, collective action with growing focus and purpose. As one example, the Druids Against Fracking group has created a public sigil, engaged in various demonstrations and activity, all to stop fracking globally. In a second example, Dana and the members of the Ancient Order of Druids in America (AODA) have made an order-wide commitment to shift their seasonal rituals at the solstices and equinoxes to focus on land, sea, sky, and human community blessing and healing. AODA now organizes these rituals for their members, encouraging all members to do a basic healing and blessing ceremony that is framed by a core ritual that all members practice and share. The flexible framework encourages members to adapt the rituals to their circumstances, do the rituals in a flexible timeframe around the summer and winter solstice and spring and fall equinox, and also invite others to participate. AODA also offers an online map and an online debrief discussion for members who are participating to share and learn from each other. These two examples are one of many that are emerging as more and more people are recognizing the need to engage in larger, collective action.

What if we could use ceremony to ReVision the world? How would we even go about doing such a thing? Well, instead of being human-centric, we might want to start by using some of the lessons in this book around animism, respect, asking for permission, and start with co-creating ceremonies with the spirits of the land and with the earth itself as we describe below.

What might these ceremonies look like? We believe that these kinds of ceremonies can take many different forms and fit many different kinds of needs. They may be individual, done in small groups, or done in larger groups, gatherings, and more. Here, we offer some suggestions for things to consider:

Co-creating intentions with nature is an approach that we highly recommend be used for at least some rituals and ceremonies for the earth that you will be developing. If the ritual is on behalf of the living earth or tied to the land in any way, take time to collaboratively set intentions with the living earth. This is not always a simple process and may take quite a bit of time. Begin this with a conversation that is open to the spirits of nature. Rather than saying, "I want to do this ritual," instead, go to nature and simply say, "What do you need?" "How can I support you?" and see what comes from that conversation. Don't assume you know what the spirits of the land want and need, but rather, allow the spirits of nature to collaborate with you to co-create the ritual. You can also reach out and say, "I'd like to offer a healing ritual for the land. Would this be welcome? If so, how can we proceed together?" The point here is that if you go in telling the land what you are already planning on doing, that's not very reciprocal. Rather, create space for a conversation and a shared vision to come forth. Use all of your intuition and spirit communication to do so!

Inviting Others. We have found that doing these ceremonies with others—and inviting others to participate and lend their energy—is highly effective. As the challenges we face are collective and involve all human beings, the more humans that can be present for these kinds of ceremonies, the better! Remember that, as we covered in chapter 3: "Rewilding," ceremonies do not need to be stuffy, scripted, or overtly esoteric. These ceremonies can be simply people coming together to sing and honor the land.

Responding to ongoing issues. Another option for rituals is to get a group together for healing and blessing that can respond to global events that harm the land and her communities. These may be oil spills, wildfires, floods, drought, tsunamis, hurricanes, and other environmental challenges that are brought on by the age of the Anthropocene.

Regular ceremonies. Consider how you might build a regular cycle of ceremonies into your own practices—perhaps you pick the full moons, the equinoxes and solstices (as AODA does) or some other regular cyclical approach. Just like earth has a cycle, so too, do effective ceremonies happen with some regularity.

HOLDING AND CRAFTING A SACRED VISION AND TELLING A BETTER STORY

What does it mean to have a vision for the future? You might think of a vision as a plan or set of principles, principles that you can use to make life choices, share with others, and work to bring into the world around you. That is, it is a guiding mantra for you to envision a brighter tomorrow and replace the visions of death, despair, and hopelessness that we have been given. And that's why we call this chapter *ReVisioning*—because we are consciously choosing to change the dystopian vision that has been given to us and create a better vision, and thus, change the future from one of fear to one of hope.

As you begin to think about this visioning work, it is important to recognize what makes the magic of visioning fruitful. The first key aspect is about empowerment and believing that you can make powerful change. We have been culturally disempowered, instead putting our power and sovereignty in the hands of experts. Don't wait for someone else to fix it because that someone may never arrive. Instead, take steps to fix it yourself, in your own way, in the places that you can reach and impact. Take back your sovereignty and make a better life for yourself and future generations. That's the real power of visioning—it is making a decision to do something, to see a better way forward, and to enact that in your community.

The second part of the magic is that this, in fact, is magical work. It is metaphysical, it impacts the material world but functions differently. Thus, believing in that power, raising and channeling energy, working with others who are committed—this is part of visioning that will allow us all to change the world. The first step is believing we can make these changes through magical means, and the second step is doing the visioning work.

The third part of the magic is tied to working with others who are committed. Who you are doing this visioning with: are you working with yourself? A small community? A group of friends and/or family who are looking to build a better tomorrow? Your spiritual community? The spirits of nature and the land around you? We suggest inviting as many others as possible into this visioning process; there is power in numbers, and the more people that take up this work now, the more powerful our vision—and future reality—will be. There is a traditional teaching that when three or more are gathered together in spiritual work, the effects are vastly amplified.

Another part of the magic of visioning is the scope: visions are often grand, big, and not always easily attainable. These visions may not happen in your lifetime, but the act of articulating a vision and working toward it itself is a powerful magical act. Don't try to fit your vision into what is achievable now, but rather, recognize that these kinds of visions take time. Give yourself permission to envision the best future you can—don't let our current views of how we live or limitations about the power of this work stop you from weaving the magic of that grand vision for the future. Dream big, dream beautifully, and dream creatively.

As we begin to get into the deep work of ReVisioning, we also want to talk about the past–present–future stories in the first six chapters. These stories are models for visioning. In the six stories, we've offered a description of the past and the challenges we face: we've offered the present—which we've visioned as hopeful and as a turning point; and we've offered our best possible vision of the future. These stories have power and as they grow and are read by you, they will take on a spirit and energy of their own. If that spirit is nurtured, the vision can grow and expand.

Storytelling and Visioning

One magical act of visioning is found through storytelling. Storytelling is powerful and can be done with humans in small or large group settings, or even with nonhuman persons like rivers, trees, or animals. This visioning is for us to simply create and share powerful stories—stories of the world we want to see, stories of the work in the world we want to do, and stories of how we all become the best ancestors that we can be. As we explored throughout this book, these stories are as old as time itself—and there's nothing needed other than to get a group to sit around a fire or a comfortable living room and simply share what is on their minds and hearts. These stories are powerful, meaningful, and can create change.

Looking at another aspect of this work, it can be valuable to look back on the stories that have powerfully influenced your own life. They can be fiction stories, nonfiction stories, personal stories, legends, myths, books, movies or shows. What are the visions behind these stories? How did they speak to you? Why were they powerful? What impact did they have on you and why?

Now, reflect on the stories you want to share and why. It can be very helpful to share specific hopeful stories of things that are happening now or have happened recently that are making a difference in the world whether it's on a small, personal scale or it's having a larger global, more powerful impact. Share any stories that come to you. Write these stories down, find ways of weaving them into what you do, share them with others in whatever way you feel led. Invite others into the storytelling, as a hopeful vision process.

As an example of the power of storytelling and visioning, we'll return briefly to the story of Clear Creek, which Dana wrote about in chapter 4: "Regeneration." After writing the story with the vision of the healed and loved creek, Dana took the story and read it to Sulphur/Clear Creek. The Creek loved the story and found joy and hope in it. Ever since then, when Dana drives by or stops to see the future Clear Creek, the Creek is full of positive energy and joy and the Creek physically looks healthier. When she goes to visit the creek, Dana spends time reinforcing the vision. She stands in front of the creek as it is, but in her mind's eye, she holds the vision powerfully of what the creek will be. And every time she reads the story, it brings tears to her eyes and she is filled with hope. Writing and sharing this story has fundamentally changed the energy and hope surrounding the creek—and will bring that vision to reality. She has begun doing this on a broader scale throughout her home in the Laurel Highlands of western Pennsylvania and has invited others to do the same. What we've just described is the power of storytelling, and some of these sharing and manifestation techniques are further explored later in this section.

Collaborative Visioning with Human and Nonhuman Others

After you've spent some time telling stories and opening yourself up to this work, you might continue by reflecting or meditating on the following questions to help shape a specific vision by yourself, with others, and with nature (see next section). A meditative tool that can be very helpful is discursive meditation: it is a kind of focused, directed thinking where you enter a meditative state (using breathwork, relaxation, clearing your mind) and then carefully think through the question. If you find yourself going too far off into a different topic, simply trace your steps back to your original question and keep thinking through. You can use this technique to explore the following questions in a meaningful, deep way:

- What are the problems you see at present that are most pressing to you personally? To your community? To the earth where you live? To the world? (Note: you don't have to dwell on this, but it's a good idea to have a clear sense of problems.

It is easier to understand solutions when you understand what you are facing.)

- What are inspirations for you at present? That is, what things that you see are going in what you consider the "right" direction for the future? Can you take that "right direction" further?
- What gives you the most hope?
- What kind of world do you want to live in? What are things that could make that happen?
- What do you see as the role of humans in relationship to the land?
- What do you see as the role of nature in relationship to humans?
- What kind of world do you want to leave behind?
- What would be better than what is currently happening?
- What is a bright future you can get excited about?

You may also realize that as you are doing this work, you don't have all the answers. That's okay. Visioning takes time—and taking the first few steps on that journey is the idea now.

In addition to using these questions for meditation, the questions listed can be powerful when used in a community setting. You can ask the questions and then take turns to share insights and engage in deep listening with each other to help shape a broader vision that can be shared by humans in your immediate circle. This can be complimented by storytelling.

Co-creating a sacred vision with the spirits of nature and the living earth is another important part of visioning as we are working to weave the threads of humanity, nature, and spirit back together. As humans are now the driving force on this planet (the "anthro" in the age of the Anthropocene, the current age of human-driven global change), it is important that visions of the future are not created for nature by humans, but collaboratively with nature. We don't want to assume we know what is best for nature or that we have all the answers—this kind of thinking is what we are fighting against.

To co-create stories with nature, the general practice is simple, drawn from our earlier discussions on animism and spirit interaction in chapter 2 and communicating with spirits of place in chapter 6. Go out into your local landscape and using the same questions or similar questions above, ask the spirits of nature to respond. Then have a conversation, use divination, or any other means to set those intentions. It may take some time as nature often works on a different timeline than we do. But this work will unfold and you'll see how rich the collaborative intention setting can be.

Ultimately, one of the things you can do when collaborative visioning is to see yourself as a vessel for these positive visions of the future, supported and enriched by the spirits of nature, to come into manifestation.

Visioning Through the 7 R's

Another framework through which to explore visioning is through the seven R's. Just as each of our chapters offered the stories surrounding the theme, you might use the seven R's to explore different aspects of your vision. You can consider the following:

- How do I envision a future that embraces rewilding?
- What does my future, rewilded self look like?
- What are thc first steps on that journey to that good future?

We used the term "rewilding" above as an example, but you can use these same questions as prompts for the other R's: reconnection, respect, rewilding, regeneration, resilience, reenchantment, and ReVisioning. Here you may note that we've not only included an outer vision (visioning the future for humans/nature) but also one for yourself: what does your best future self look like? This, too, is a powerful transformative act that allows you to be the best person you can be.

Holding and Radiating a Vision into the World in the Metaphysical Realms

As we began to see with the last section on creative practices and finding audiences, and in Dana's story of sharing the vision with Sulphur/Clear Creek, visions are more powerful when shared. Once you have that vision, even if it's incomplete or evolving, it is critical to begin to share that vision and spread it in any way you can—and there are both metaphysical and physical approaches to do so.

Holding and radiating a vision metaphysically is also critical—and we've explored this already through ceremonies in this chapter. As we have explored throughout this book, there is a power not only in manifesting in the material realm but in magical work surrounding the vision. A simple practice that you can do involves holding the vision in your mind as often and as strongly as you can. You can do this as part of your meditative practices. For example, one way Dana uses in her regular spiritual practices as a Druid land healer is to provide a vision of a healthy and rich ecosystem. So, she will go into the most damaged places, like a logged forest or where a mountaintop has been removed, and she will envision a future where the land is healed, healthy, whole, and tended in a loving manner. Envisioning the monoculture crops of cornfields and lawns instead as abundant polycultures of berries, fruit, nuts with a bounty of animal and insect life, for example. This is a simple and yet extremely powerful magical practice you can do and integrate this practice into your regular spiritual work.

As we explored above, you can also do this visioning work ceremonially—where a group of humans and/or nature spirits get together to help vision this, creating and layering the vision, and holding it as strongly as they can, radiating that vision outward into the land.

LIVING, SHARING, AND BROADENING THE VISION

A final method of bringing the magic of visioning into reality is to bring the metaphysical down into the physical realm, by doing something to bring the vision to life with your own hands, heart, and mind. Any magical work, but certainly visioning work, is more effective when we do both the inner and outer work. A vision of the future is like a seed—we are planting the seed that has the potential to germinate, break through the soil, and grow into a beautiful oak tree. But in order for the seed to germinate and grow, that seed needs the right conditions: light, moisture, nutrient-rich soil, and warmth. Visions are the same—as you breathe energy into a vision, it comes alive. As you strengthen that vision and continue to share it and grow it with a community, the spirit of the vision grows stronger. Then, the vision makes a transition to the material world—and by doing something material toward that vision, even if it is the smallest step, you are bringing it into the physical world. The vision continues to grow and gain strength and soon becomes a towering oak.

Thus, we will now explore actions in the world, and how we can bring forth grand transformations of human society that shifts us back into a nurturing, care-oriented society that connects to nature and spirit. As we've described above, our book has offered the seven R's to rethink human society and our relationship with the earth and spirit: reconnection, respect, rewilding, regeneration, resilience, reenchantment, and now, ReVisioning. And in this book, we've offered plenty of ways that you can begin to bring these themes into your life and into your family and community. This is our vision—a general map, set of tools, and place to begin for you to create and craft your own. The seven R's are the broader framework, but the specific details are up to you.

STEPS ON THE PATH TO THE BRIGHT FUTURE

How might you begin to walk the path toward your future vision? What steps do you need to take, what choices do you need to make, and what things do you need to embrace or shift in order for that to happen? In small, slow ways, find ways of living the vision you have created. A thousand small, slow solutions can end up to massive changes over time. As you bring these visions into your own life, something else can occur—you can start seeing your life transform. These kinds of changes may include changing lifestyles, moving or forming an intentional community, learning how to tend and regenerate land, learning wildtending practices, learning how to live more simply, planting trees, and so on. Through these transformative and healing actions, you can change your own life and change the world.

Sharing the Vision

Once you are living the vision or doing something, share the vision. Share it however you can, in whatever communities you have access to. Invite people in to co-create the vision through storytelling, arts, and other creative practices. Build a movement. Bring people together for ceremonies, to talk, share, and grow. Create change.

Creating and Sharing Vision Through Bardic Practices

Just as the Hollywood blockbusters share dystopian visions of the future, so too can you leverage creative practices to share a hopeful, positive vision of the future. Using the practices above, you can use the bardic arts to help get the message out.

Start by thinking about the specific kind of art (bardic work) you produce and what kinds of messages you can share. Certain art forms are easier to convey messages than others. When you convey messages in your work, can the work stand on its own, or do you want to share some information about the work in addition to the work itself?

Consider your specific messages or themes you want to convey. Perhaps you have a very specific message or a general one. Think about the thing you most would like to see in the world—write it down and keep it in mind when you create. With your work, consider presenting a general philosophy about your work. Messaging can come in a lot of forms: these sometimes come in the form of "artist statements" that talk about your work and inspirations or may come through the words, songs, or dances themselves. This is especially helpful for work that can be interpreted in many ways, or whose interpretation is not immediately clear upon examination (e.g., woodcarving or dance). You can share these messages on social media, on your website, even with the physical art that someone receives.

Creative practices are an excellent way to share a vision about the future with others in your immediate area or sphere of influence. Consider who you can reach and how you can reach them. Perhaps this is a local exhibit or show, a poetry slam, or through social media. Consider your audience and what messages may be most appropriate for you to share in this visionary way.

For example, as Dana has shared in chapter 4, she lives in a region of the USA that is currently a fossil fuel and natural resource extraction zone: with fracking, acid mine drainage, mountaintop removal, unsustainable logging, coal-fired power plants, toxic waste, and hunting for sport. Where she lives, most people view nature as something to extract; a resource to be profited from, and a way to keep jobs in the region. Thus, there is very little respect or love for nature—so the art that she shares locally offers a different message. Dana has had several opportunities to hang artwork in high traffic areas, such as at a regional hospital. This body of work she shares focuses on offering an alternative view of the land, shifting away from resource extraction and into reconnection, regeneration, and rewilding. She painted trees with hearts in the ground, she painted the telluric currents of earth energy flowing in a healthy way, and she painted regenerated and wild landscapes. The works were accompanied by short paragraphs that described these visions. The more these kinds of alternative messages and perspectives can get into circulation, the more "normalized" they become and the more power they hold. These paintings told a very different tale than the land outside that continued to be extracted—and they had impact.

Providing alternative perspectives, enchantment, and visioning for the future is certainly a magical act and one that many people who practice the bardic arts might build into their work. When you create something and put it out in the world, you have an opportunity to create so much more than just a piece of art, music, dance—it offers hope.

Broader Scale Vision and Connecting to Similar Movements

Once we have the vision, the next step is redesigning and revising our current human societies. While this sounds like an enormous task, just hear us out! The very good news is that we are seeing a lot of movement in these directions already, even if you aren't seeing this movement in the major headlines. Through different communities, all across the land, people are realigning their relationships with the land and the spirits of nature. This work is growing, spreading, and deepening from a multitude of different places, peoples, and practices. We can see these shifts in ecological design and growing practices like permaculture, natural building, restoration agriculture, and the rise of local food movements. We see it in alternative health movements such as through herbalism and sacred movement practices. We see it in the sharp rise of practitioners of nature spirituality such as through druidry, green witchcraft, shamanism, and broader neopaganism. Even monotheistic religions are starting to talk more about earth care and making it a more central part of their tradition. We see it in alternative living communities, such as ecovillages, tiny houses, and earthships where people are taking radical approaches to living ecologically and close to the land. Everywhere you turn, more and more people are finding their way back into a sacred relationship not only with nature but with the spirits of nature. This realignment work is necessary if we are going to create a better vision of the future and fight for the right of *all* life on this planet to thrive.

To begin, you might seek models of lifestyles and living that already are out there and connect to some communities already doing this work or parts of it. Go visit an ecovillage or alternative housing community. Spend time with teachers of ancestral skills. Learn and practice permaculture and rewilding. Seek the people who are already walking in a similar path and learn.

A NEW PARADIGM EMERGING

All of this visioning leads us to share our understanding of what we see as an emerging new paradigm for the present and future. A paradigm is a set of patterns including thoughts, actions, beliefs, and practices, under which people operate. As we have explored in the past stories in this book, we were all born into the destructive paradigms of our current age: where money, colonization, domination, and the myth of progress are embedded into the foundations of our current civilization. This paradigm is replicated and interwoven in nearly everything our present civilization produces: from mass industrial agriculture to mass education, from big government and big corporations to the exploitation of native peoples and environmental degradation. And yet, the core values of the paradigm (greed, growth at all costs, narcissism, efficiency, progress) are often unarticulated and yet influencing our thoughts, lives, and actions.

What we have been offering in this book is a new paradigm, a paradigm for the future that helps us reindigenize to place, reconnect, rewild, and ultimately, reenchant the world.

As we shared in the introduction, the foundations for the new paradigm have been being laid by many people for decades and Indigenous communities have, in many cases, never lost this wisdom. But for many of us growing up in Western civilization, it is a lifeline to something better. The new paradigm does not yet have a name, or rather, the paradigm has many different names. But everywhere you look—from herbalism schools to earth skills events to community gardens to natural arts—the new paradigm is growing in strength. Each of us individually saw this paradigm taking shape in the many communities to which we belong and were excited to see the overlaps—how different groups engaging in very different practices who had literally no connection with each other are still coming to similar values and practices. That regardless of where you go, so many of the same conversations—the conversations we've tackled in this book—are taking place. As we have shared in the introduction: this is not our paradigm—it belongs to all of us. What we have attempted to do in this book is to offer an overall road map and set of practices to get us there through the 7 R's. Now we will present it in a different way, through the values, practices, and experiences that we are seeing and building collectively and in an exciting way.

Values are what we hold to be important, of worth, and also the standards to which we can hold ourselves to particular sets of right behavior. **Practices** are these values enacted, which vary considerably by community, but as you will see, consensus does emerge. **Outcomes** are some of the things we are seeing happen and change as the new paradigm comes into being, even in small ways.

Values: Reconnection and Respect

The primary value of the new paradigm is an affirmation that the earth is our home and mother and all life on earth should be nurtured, honored, and acknowledged. All life on earth has a right to exist, and part of re-indigenizing to place is learning how to work in a respectful way to honor all life and also meet human needs. Tied to this primary value are respectful interactions for all beings, human or otherwise. The foundations include the following values:

- Knowing that the earth can provide for our needs and recognizing the value of learning the skills through which to connect with the earth

- Emphasizing holistic understandings of ourselves and the world around us. For human beings, this includes acknowledging and connecting mind, body, spirit, and the need for healing/growth/attention on all three levels

- Recognizing our own interconnectedness to all life and our place in the broader ecosystem and on a planet-wide scale

- Recognizing that the world is an incredibly alive, enchanted, and magical place

- Recognizing that as humans, we have a lot to learn and many ways to grow: learning skills of deep listening, self-reflection, action, and awareness so that we can address our own biases and embrace a mindset that allows us to learn from our mistakes and keep growing in ways that are honest, open, and meaningful.

- Affirming that the Earth is sacred and should be honored and respected, including acknowledging all life on earth as sovereign and the earth herself as a sovereign being

- Acknowledging the ancestors of the land and the value of Indigenous teachings and ways of knowing

- Recognizing that humans can be a force of healing and good in the world and that we all can make that happen individually and on a community-wide level and that this work can be nourishing and joyful

- Recognizing that care is a foundation of interactions between humans, nature, and spirit

Practices: Rewilding, Regeneration, Resilience

Practices are values in action; they allow us to manifest these value systems in the world around us to enact change, live differently, and engage in different kinds of activity. Practices are our best attempts to manifest the growing value system of this new paradigm and often appear differently in different communities and with different individuals depending on the focus.

- Offering gratitude for each other and for the land in all things and in multiple ways: Practicing reciprocation and interaction with the earth to recognize that we need to both give and take for the earth to be fruitful and abundant.
- Being in community with each other and working hard toward cultivating healthy communities
- Cultivating and honoring diverse peoples, bodies, beliefs, and abilities through words and actions
- Rejecting the common stereotypes, consumption-driven behaviors, and identities of capitalist culture and embracing individual expression and identity
- Learning some set of skills in a collaborative and community-supported setting with often very accessible, nurturing, and low-stakes teaching practices.
- Cultivating practices that honor our own intuition, creativity, and individual skills
- Practicing sustainable and regenerative approaches where the emphasis is on being local, situated, and reciprocal including localizing connection to the earth and meeting one's needs, gathering or growing local materials
- Attending to creating and building specific, contextualized, and local knowledge and honoring the differences in ecosystems or people.
- Using technology in ethical ways, embracing appropriate technologies, and valuing the role of human labor over fossil fuels and human thought and creativity over technologically generated thought, words, and ideas
- Emphasizing whole systems thinking, and thinking in cycles and in longer time frames, mirroring the patterns of nature.

- Functioning in slow time, where there is an emphasis on doing things well rather than quickly or efficiently

- Engaging in ceremony for each other and for the earth.

- Actively regenerating and healing the earth through gardens, food forests, rewilding landscapes, and more.

- Teaching younger generations the values, practices, outcomes, and the 7 R's.

Outcomes: Reenchantment and ReVisioning

Can you imagine a world that was fueled by the above values and practices rather than one that is fueled by the myth of progress and human narcissism? We certainly can, and a growing number of other people can as well! This movement is growing person by person, day by day, and all it takes is enough of us with the vision to bring it firmly into reality as the new paradigm for our planet. And with the values and practices shared above and throughout this book, we can have everything we vision and more:

- Experiencing a sense of deep belonging or homecoming as they begin to find communities who do these practices and take them up themselves. And when this immersion is temporary (such as going to an event for a week and then returning to "normal live") having a "hard return" when you come back where shifting back into the old paradigm can be disturbing, unbalancing, and depressing

- Interacting with the spirits of nature and have a range of profound experiences with nature that are embodied, joyful, and meaningful

- Experiencing a landscape full of green wisdom, spirit teachers, magic, and enchantment

- Coming together in communities to do good work, support each other, learn, and have a sense of belonging and meaning.

- Observing a healed, bountiful landscape full of life and joy, where all needs can be met and there is more than enough abundance for all

- Witnessing damaged ecosystems regenerate and the profound healing power of nature reshape damaged places into healed ones; through this participation, allowing that same healing force of nature to work within ourselves
- Recognizing our own place in the earth as caretakers and guardians of the land

INVITATION TO ACTION: WRITING YOUR OWN FUTURE

When you are inspired by some great purpose, some extraordinary project, all your thoughts break their bonds; your mind transcends limitations; your conscious expands in every direction; and you find yourself in a great, new and wonderful world.

—PATANJALI, THE YOGA SUTRAS

As we've said before, this entire book is a work of magic. It is a ceremony, a magical story, and a spell all wrapped up in one. But it won't actually work unless you participate. To weave a better future, as many people as possible together need to ReVision that brighter, earth-centered, and healed future. Not just Dana, not just Nate. You and your community as well.

Our new paradigm is like a river system. Each of us is a spring, a stream, a small contribution. As we move and flow together, our springs and streams become the creeks and rivers of our communities, flowing into larger rivers, and eventually, flowing into a massive river like the Mississippi River. Then, we have so much movement forward, we see change across the land. Recognize you alone don't have to be the Mississippi—but in your own way, you can contribute to that flow and movement in a better, more hopeful direction. You can join in building a new paradigm for the future, one that replaces the worn-out and tired one of the present that no longer serves us.

In this book, we've done our best to combat the dystopian, dark apocalyptic vision that keeps getting pushed onto us. We've shared a different vision, a different story, and perhaps just as importantly, we've shared tools and a road map to changing that—by bringing people, nature, and the world of spirit into equal harmony, we can shift humanity's relationship with nature to one of balance. We can integrate humans, nature, and spirit in powerful ways. So, what are you waiting for?

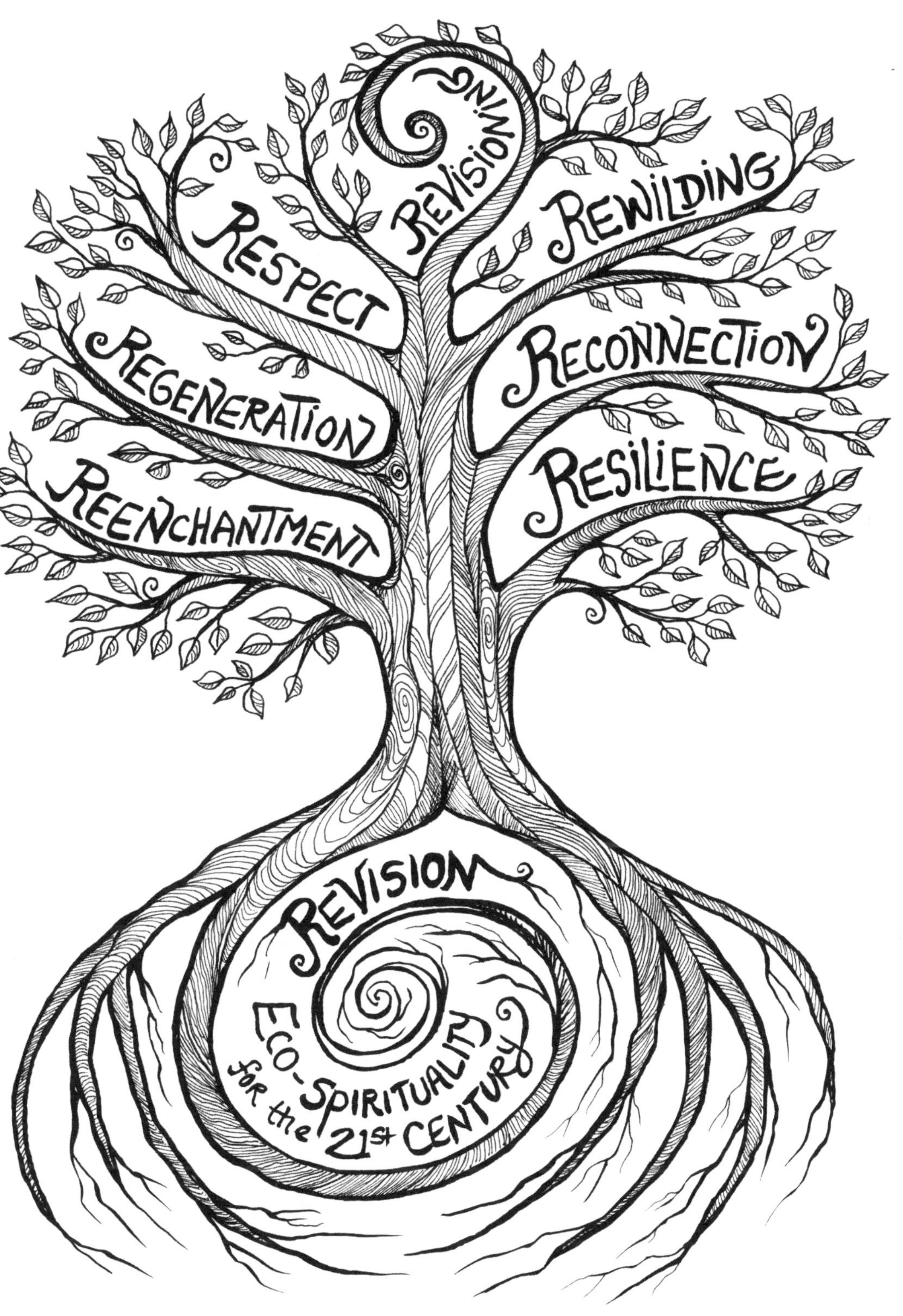
ReVisioning
Respect
Rewilding
Regeneration
Reconnection
Reenchantment
Resilience
ReVision
Eco-Spirituality for the 21st Century

Endnotes

1. There are a number of dystopian fiction books and movies in this paragraph, including George Orwell's *1984* (first published in 1949), Aldous Huxley's *Brave New World* (published in 1932), Margaret Atwood's *Handmaid's Tale* (book, 1985; TV series, 2017), George R. R. Martin's *Game of Thrones* series (books, 1996; TV, 2011), *Breaking Bad* (TV, 2008), and *The Walking Dead* (2010).

2. More information on the Ancient Order of Druids in America can be found at www.aoda.org.

3. Dennis Meadows and Jorgan Randers, *The Limits to Growth: The 30-Year Update* (Routledge, 2012).

4. Robin Kimmerer, *Braiding Sweetgrass: Indigenous Wisdom, Scientific Knowledge, and the Teachings of Plants* (Milkweed, 2013).

5. The Tracker School is continued in the legacy of Tom Brown Jr. at https://www.trackerschool.com/.

6. A list of many earth skills gatherings and schools can be found at http://earthskillsgathering.org/.

7. James E. Lovelock, "Gaia as Seen Through the Atmosphere," in *Biomineralization and Biological Metal Accumulation: Biological and Geological Perspectives Papers*, presented at the Fourth International Symposium on Biomineralization, Renesse, The Netherlands, June 2–5, 1982 (Dordrecht, The Netherlands: Springer Netherlands, 1983), 15–25.

8. John Richards, *The Unending Frontier: An Environmental History of the Early Modern World* (University of California Press, 2003).

9. One visual example of the extent to which the world has been colonized can be found on Vox from 2014: https://www.vox.com/2014/6/24/5835320/map-in-the-whole-world-only-these-five-countries-escaped-european.

10. *Merriam-Webster Dictionary*, s.v., "Respect (noun, verb)," accessed March 21, 2023, https://www.merriam-webster.com/dictionary/respect.

11. For a full copy of the Haudenosaunee Thanksgiving address, you can download it from the Smithsonian US National Museum of the American Indian, https://americanindian.si.edu/environment/pdf/01_02_Thanksgiving_Address.pdf. For more on Thanksgiving by Jake Swamp, see *Giving Thanks: A Native American Good Morning Message* (Lee and Low Books, 1997).

12. Dana's book *Sacred Actions: Living the Wheel of the Year Through Earth-Centered Sustainable Practices* (REDFeather, 2021) is full of suggestions for this work.

13. Patricia Robin Woodruff, *Roots of Slavic Magic Book 1: Slavic Deities & Their Worship* (Patricia Robin Woodruff, 2024).

14. For a good overview of animism both present and ancient, see *Animism: Respecting the Living World* by Graham Harvey (Wakefield, 2005).

15. Tyson Yunkaporta, *Sand Talk: How Indigenous Thinking Can Save the World* (Text Publishing, 2019).

16. *Inhabit: A Permaculture Perspective* (film). More details at http://inhabitfilm.com/.

17. Kimmerer, *Braiding Sweetgrass*.

18. In Nate's book *Primal: Why We Long to Be Wild and Free* (Falcon Guides, 2019), he explores the stories of how many people are seeking more wild, free practices and connections with nature.

19. For more on the revitalization of Chernobyl, see the UN Environment Programme's article "How Chernobyl Has Become an Unexpected Haven for Wildlife," https://www.unep.org/news-and-stories/story/how-chernobyl-has-become-unexpected-haven-wildlife.

20. For more on building a relationship with fire, see Nate's book *Awakening Fire: An Essential Guide to Waking Flame, Wood, and Ignition* (Falcon Guides, 2021).

21. Albrecht I. Schulte-Hostedde, Zvia Mazal, Claire M. Jardine, and Jeffrey Gagnon, "Enhanced Access to Anthropogenic Food Waste Is Related to Hyperglycemia in Raccoons (Procyon lotor)," *Conservation Physiology* 6, no. 1 (2018): 26.

22. Some of my recommendations in this regard include the incredible content found in *Plant Healer Magazine*, the *Earthwise Herbal* vols. 1 & 2 by Matthew Wood, and Jim McDonald's Lindera: Four Seasons Herbalism Course.

23. This point is critical. For more information on the different practices of land healing, please see Dana's *Land Healing: Physical and Metaphysical Regeneration of the Earth*.

24. Data on land use in the United States come from Dave Merrill and Lauren Leatherby's "How America Uses Its Land," Bloomburg, July 31, 2018, https://www.bloomberg.com/graphics/2018-us-land-use/.

25. Wendell Berry, *The Unsettling of America: Culture and Agriculture* (Counterpoint, rev. ed., 2004; original publication was in 1977).

26. D. L. Driscoll, *Channeling the Awen Within: An Exploratory Study of the Bardic Arts in the Modern Druid Tradition* (Order of Bards, Ovates, and Druids, 2018), https://druidry.org/resources/the-nineteenth-mount-haemus-lecture.

27. A great overview of alternative economics can be found on the Free Permaculture website, https://www.freepermaculture.com/regenerative-economics/.

28. Vicki Robin and Joe Dominguez, *Your Money or Your Life: 9 Steps to Transforming Your Relationship with Money and Achieving Financial Independence; Fully Revised and Updated for 2018* (Penguin, 2008).

29. Carl Jung, *Aion: Researches into the Phenomenology of the Self*, trans. R. F. C. Hull (Princeton, NJ: Princeton University Press, 1969).

30. Abdolali Mohagheghzadeh, Pouya Faridi, Mohammadreza Shams-Ardakani, and Younes Ghasemi, "Medicinal Smokes," *Journal of Ethnopharmacology* 108, no. 2 (2006): 161–84.

31. Carol S. Dweck, *Mindset: The New Psychology of Success* (Random House, 2006).

32. Barry Glassner, "Culture of Fear and the Presidential Scare," *Contexts* 19, no. 1 (2020): 68–68.

33. For more on body radar and other scoutcraft skills, please see Nate Summers, *Shadow Survival: A Guide to Tactical Awareness, Camouflage, Evasion, Advanced Survival, and More*, Scoutcraft 1 (Nate Summers, 2024).

34. Robert Alexander Weinstein, *The Master Plant Teachers: A Spiritual Journey into the World of Amazonian Plant Medicine and Tibetan Buddhism* (2022).

35. Jon Young shared this in conversation with me; he was a friend of Bill Munroe.

36. Peter Tompkins and Christopher Bird, *The Secret Life of Plants: A Fascinating Account of the Physical, Emotional, and Spiritual Relations Between Plants and Man* (Harper and Row, 1989).

37. For ayahuasca ditea plant fasts, I recommend Robert Weinstein's *The Master Plant Teachers*, and for more on utiseta, I would consider Kaldera's *Wightridden: Paths of Northern Tradition Shamanism* (Asphodel, 2007).

38. Vine Deloria Jr., *The World We Used to Live In: Remembering the Powers of the Medicine Men* (Fulcrum, 2006).

39. Matthew Hilton, "Consumers and the State Since the Second World War," *Annals of the American Academy of Political and Social Science* 611 (2007): 66–81, http://www.jstor.org/stable/25097909.

40. Bradford Keeney, ed., *Ropes to God: Experiencing the Bushman Spiritual Universe*, vol. 8 (Leete's Island Books, 2003).

41. David Graeber and David Wengrow, *The Dawn of Everything: A New History of Humanity* (Penguin UK, 2021).

About the Authors

Dana O'Driscoll is an animist druid and permaculture practitioner with over 20 years of experience and currently serves as grand archdruid in the Ancient Order of Druids in America (aoda.org). She is the author of *Sacred Actions: Living the Wheel of the Year through Earth-Centered Spiritual Practices*, *The Sacred Actions Journal*, and *Land Healing*.

Nate Summers is a survival skills and ancestral skills teacher with over 20 years' experience teaching people from all over the world. He is the author of *Primal: Why We Long to Be Wild and Free* (2019) and *Shadow Survival* (2024).

Library of Congress Control Number: 2025930183

Designed by Alexa Harris
Cover and interior art by Dana O'Driscoll
Type set in Square Peg / Palomino Sans One / Bressay
Photo by Annie Spratt on Unsplash

ISBN: 978-0-7643-7016-8
ePub: 978-1-5073-0590-4
Printed in China

10 9 8 7 6 5 4 3 2 1

Published by REDFeather Mind, Body, Spirit
An imprint of Schiffer Publishing, Ltd.
4880 Lower Valley Road
Atglen, PA 19310
Phone: (610) 593-1777; Fax: (610) 593-2002
Email: Info@redfeathermbs.com
Web: www.redfeathermbs.com